PALEO KIDS LUNCH BREAK

35 KID-APPROVED SNACK AND LUNCH-TIME RECIPES THAT ARE DELICIOUS, LOW-COST, AND EASY-TO-MAKE

EVA ILIANA

CONTENTS

Introduction: The Paleo Diet for Your Whole Family — 5

1. Eating Like Cavemen—What Is It All About? — 13
2. Adapting Paleo for Kids — 36
3. Strength in Numbers—Bringing Your Whole Family on Board — 61
4. Lunch Is Served! — 87
5. Snacks Your Kids Will Enjoy — 145
6. Bringing the Paleo Diet to Life for the Long Run — 187

Conclusion: Going Paleo With Your Family — 209
References — 213

© **Copyright 2020 - All rights reserved.**

The content contained within this book may not be reproduced, duplicated or transmitted without direct written permission from the author or the publisher.

Under no circumstances will any blame or legal responsibility be held against the publisher, or author, for any damages, reparation, or monetary loss due to the information contained within this book, either directly or indirectly.

Legal Notice:

This book is copyright protected. It is only for personal use. You cannot amend, distribute, sell, use, quote or paraphrase any part, or the content within this book, without the consent of the author or publisher.

Disclaimer Notice:

Please note the information contained within this document is for educational and entertainment purposes only. All effort has been executed to present accurate, up to date, reliable, complete information. No warranties of any kind are declared or implied. Readers acknowledge that the author is not engaged in the rendering of legal, financial, medical or professional advice. The content within this book has been derived from various sources. Please consult a licensed professional before attempting any techniques outlined in this book.

By reading this document, the reader agrees that under no circumstances is the author responsible for any losses, direct or indirect, that are incurred as a result of the use of the information contained within this document, including, but not limited to, errors, omissions, or inaccuracies.

INTRODUCTION: THE PALEO DIET FOR YOUR WHOLE FAMILY

Fig. 1: Family Dinner. Unsplash, by Pablo Merchán Montes, 2018, https://unsplash.com/photos/wYOPqmtDD0w/ Copyright 2018 by Pablo Merchán Montes/Unsplash.

"A healthy outside starts from the inside."

— URICH

Can you guess what the best diet for your child is?

As a parent, hearing the words "diet for kids" may sound a little strange, unless your child is suffering from obesity and their pediatrician has recommended they lose weight to avoid the risk of developing chronic conditions. Another possible scenario that could lead to this is if you and your partner follow the same diet or lifestyle. For instance, if you are a vegan, there is a high chance you'll raise your children as vegans, too. Aside from the reasons above, you might not see the essence of placing your child on a specific diet. But if you're reading this eBook right now, it means you're interested in a very specific diet—the Paleolithic or, simply, "Paleo" diet.

I can strongly recall the instance when I decided to place my kids on this diet. I had religiously followed Paleo for about a year and had personally experienced the numerous benefits of the diet. Whilst sitting at our dining table thinking about what to buy at the supermarket, I considered how simple life would be if my kids were on Paleo, too. After sending my kids off to school, I started researching about Paleo for kids. Much to my surprise and delight, I discovered that Paleo was one of the diets kids can follow. In fact, it provides a number of health benefits to children, also.

Although food—specifically, processed food—is readily available today, our earliest ancestors didn't have access to the variety of options we have now. The foods our ancestors **fed on** depended on their geographical conditions, the paleontological period they lived in, and the changes in the seasons. In other words, they barely had a choice—they only ate what was hunted and foraged from their environment. If they couldn't find food, they didn't eat. Despite this, our earliest ancestors never had to deal with as many diet-related health issues as we face today.

Nowadays, our kids eat whatever and whenever they want. They have gotten so used to having food readily available to them that they barely think about the importance of eating healthy. This reminds me of a time when I asked my kids about their favorite foods. They said ice cream, bacon, and basically everything that comes from their all-time favorite fast food joint. Then I asked them how they would feel about eating foods like fresh fruits, fresh vegetables, and meat, just like our earliest ancestors. Naturally, they thought I was kidding, so they just laughed. That conversation made me realize how much my kids were used to the processed, refined, convenient foods most children would never get enough of. Although I had made a conscious decision to improve my life by following the Paleo diet, I had totally forgotten about them. But now, my kids are happy with their diet and have also become healthy eaters.

Basically, the Paleo diet consists of completely healthy foods like grass-fed meat, seafood, poultry, healthy oils, seeds, and nuts. With this diet, your children will **lose their uncontrollable cravings for** processed and refined food products, as well as trans fats. As you learn more about Paleo, you will also learn how to plan your meals to make it easier for you and your kids to stick with this unique diet in the long term. Paleo is one of the most popular diets nowadays, and for good reason. Personally, I have experienced a number of health benefits by **sticking with** this diet, like overcoming prediabetes, brain fog, and bloating. I even lost my excess weight! With this diet, my kids and I also enjoy stable energy levels, we sleep better, our skin and hair are healthier, and we've noticed an overall improvement in our moods. Later, we will discuss these health benefits in detail to give you a better idea of what you and your kids should potentially look forward to by following this diet.

If you're a mom like me (or a dad) and you're either thinking of trying out Paleo or are already following this diet, you might also be thinking of placing your kids on Paleo, too. Naturally, you only want what is best for your children. Therefore, you want to learn everything you can about Paleo for kids before you get started. This is a great first step. Educating yourself about this diet, what its benefits are, and how you can safely introduce it to your kids are all essential steps to helping you find success.

Here's another great thing about Paleo that I discovered while doing my research: according to a study, following this approach for a few days can guarantee you a number of health benefits, like an improvement in glucose tolerance, blood pressure, and insulin sensitivity (Frassetto et al., 2009). The same study also showed improvements in the metabolism and circulatory system of the majority of the participants. Imagine how beneficial it would be if you stay faithful **to** it long term!

Once you know more about Paleo (don't worry, we will discuss everything in detail throughout this eBook), the next thing you will have to think about is how to overcome the challenge of introducing this distinctive diet to your children. The Paleo diet is quite different from the standard American diet, or the "traditional diet" that doesn't **require** rules. When introducing this diet to your children, try thinking about how you would introduce a new set of rules or skill to them. Start slow, be patient, and don't expect that your kids get used to it right away. Here are a few tips to begin with:

Try to look for healthier alternatives for their favorite foods. This will make it easier for the transition into Paleo.

Learn how to cook their meals and snacks so they become comfortable with the diet even at school.

Add a new food item to their menu each day. Avoid overwhelming your children by serving meals where everything is new. When you introduce something new, encourage them to try it.

If your children refuse to try a new type of food, avoid forcing them. Instead, let it go. You can reintroduce the same food after a few days and this time, pair it with something you know they like.

Consider involving your children with the meal preparation and cooking. These tasks are fun, educational, and can help your children learn how to be more open in terms of trying new food.

At some point, you will have to stop making separate meals for your children. This is when you can start enjoying Paleo as a family. Still, keep one side dish or dessert familiar to your children so they still feel like they have a choice.

It is also extremely important for you to talk about this new diet change with your children. The conversation you have with your children about Paleo depends on how old they are. For instance, if you have a younger child, you can introduce the diet with a story. Why don't you try a story about cavemen and how they used to eat? Then you can use this as a segue to introduce your plans to start them on Paleo. If you have an older child, one who already understands the concept of health, then dive right into explaining the benefits of this diet to them.

Just avoid going into the technical or scientific explanations of the benefits. Make sure your explanations are age-appropriate, to ensure your kids understand why you want them to start going Paleo. Communicating with your children this way can make the whole journey a lot easier and more positive to both parties.

As a parent who is interested in Paleo for kids, you will benefit immensely from this book. Here, you will learn more about Paleo and what it entails. Also, you will learn how to approach the introduction of this diet to your children and your whole family in a realistic and effective way. I will share tips on how you can discuss food and nutrition with your children, how to involve your family members in going Paleo, and how to maintain this diet together. I will also share with you several easy and cost-effective recipes to cook right in the comfort of your home. Learning how to cook for your kids is one of the most effective ways to stick with Paleo long-term.

By reading this eBook, you will determine the perfect transition that works best for your family. Since you already know your children's current diet and eating habits, learning everything you can about Paleo will help you make smarter and healthier choices for them. You will also gain valuable insights into the basic components to make any meal more Paleo-friendly and how to adjust your approach based on your family's needs. By the end of this eBook, you will have all the knowledge needed to guide your children on their Paleolithic diet journey. So... if you're ready, let's begin!

1

EATING LIKE CAVEMEN—WHAT IS IT ALL ABOUT?

Fig. 2: Hunter-Gatherers. Pixabay, by sgrunden, 2020, https://pixabay.com/photos/neanderthal-stone-age-caveman-4731921/ Copyright 2020 by sgrunden/Pixabay.

The Paleolithic diet is based on the eating habits of our hunter-gatherer ancestors, emphasizing the consumption of foods that would have been available to them. This is a dietary approach that consists of naturally-produced, nutrient-rich foods like lean meats, seafood, fruits, and vegetables. As much as possible, this diet avoids processed foods and food products that have been refined by modern technology. By eliminating artificial nutrient sources like dairy, grains, and refined sugars, the Paleo diet helps you avoid the most common types of food responsible for inflammation and other health issues.

Simply put, the Paleo diet is a unique kind of diet, as it is the only one in which our species is genetically adopted. This means following the diet ensures that you consume foods that are optimal for your body as they have been programmed into your DNA. Of course, most of the foods that were consumed by our ancestors do not exist anymore. But you can still follow the Paleo diet by mimicking the foods eaten by our ancestors. To do this, you would opt for whole, natural foods that aren't adulterated by modern food-producing methods.

Most people consider Dr. Loren Cordin as the originator of this diet. However, Dr. Cordin emphasizes that he wasn't the one who created it. This diet emerged out of the natural world—when our ancestors came into the world, they had to eat to survive. They were the very first ones who developed (although unintentionally) and followed the Paleo diet.

However, Dr. Cordin had a role to play in how we know the Paleo diet now. Along with a group of colleagues from the fields of anthropology, medicine, and nutrition, Dr. Cordin discovered the science that now stands as the basis of the diet today.

The Paleo diet is vastly different from the modern-day Western diet that most people follow. Most of the foods that are commonly eaten on the Western diet are modern, which means that they were only introduced recently. Such a diet is high in processed foods, vegetable oils, and refined sugar, all of which don't do anything good for the body. Unfortunately, our bodies haven't evolved enough to catch up with these modern-day foods. Because of this, we cannot digest them properly, and this is one of the reasons why it becomes difficult to make the most out of them.

But when you start following the Paleo diet, you will feel healthier and more empowered. You stay focus**ed** on nutrient-dense foods while eliminating those that commonly cause inflammation. The best part is, the Paleo diet is suitable for children, too. But since this diet is quite unique, you should learn everything you can about it before introducing it to your children. In fact, it would be better to start by following the diet yourself, and once you feel like you have a good understanding of it, you can start introducing it to your children gradually.

WHAT CAN YOU EAT?

Since this diet is primarily based on the foods that were available to our ancestors, it means you will have to eliminate most of the modern foods available to us now. Instead, you will stay committed to wild animal-based meats (lean meat, bone marrow, no dairy) and naturally-sourced plant foods (vegetables, fruits, non-grains, nuts). To give you a better idea of what this diet entails, we will discuss the foods to eat while on Paleo, as well as the foods to avoid. That way, you know how to plan your children's meals and introduce the diet in the best way possible. While following Paleo, these are the foods you (and your children) can eat:

Eggs (preferably free-range or fully-pastured)

Eggs are an excellent source of protein, healthy fats, and other nutrients that children need to grow healthy and strong. The great thing about eggs is that you can cook them in various ways and even use them in your recipes.

Fish (preferably wild-caught)

Wild-caught fish are healthier compared to the ones raised in fish farms mainly because they are leaner. Some examples include:

- anchovies

- bass
- catfish
- cod
- flatfish
- grouper
- haddock
- herring
- mackerel
- salmon
- sardines
- tilapia
- trout
- tuna
- turbot
- walleye

Fruit

Since you will be avoiding most sweets on the Paleo diet, fruits will come to the rescue as you can eat them to satisfy your sweet tooth. And since most fruits contain vitamins and minerals, they're perfect for kids! Here are some of the best examples of fruits to feed your kids on Paleo:

- apples
- bananas

- berries like blueberries, blackberries, strawberries, and raspberries
- cantaloupes
- citrus fruits like oranges, grapefruits, and tangerines
- grapes
- honeydew
- kiwis
- lychees
- peaches
- tomatoes
- watermelons

Game Meat

If you're a fan of hunting, you can catch your meat and cook it in different ways. Although these aren't common for children, you can still introduce the following types of game meat to them:

- bear
- deer
- duck
- elk
- moose
- rabbit
- reindeer

Healthy Fats

Healthy fat sources are an important part of the Paleo diet, especially for cooking. Instead of choosing processed fats, your best options are:

- avocado
- butter
- chia seeds
- coconut oil
- ghee (preferably from grass-fed butter)
- olive oil
- tahini

Herbs and Spices

Adding herbs and spices to your dishes makes them healthier and more flavorful. Aside from this, most herbs and spices have anti-inflammatory properties, making them beneficial for the entire family. Here are some examples of herbs to include in your cooking:

- basil
- cacao powder
- capers
- chilies
- chives

- cilantro
- garlic
- ginger
- leeks
- mustard
- parsley
- vinegar

Meats

Lean meats are very important on Paleo, so make sure to include these in your dishes. Try to alternate between different kinds of meat and other protein sources to keep your children interested in the diet. Some of the best types of meat for children include:

- bacon (preferably nitrate-free)
- beef (preferably grass-fed)
- lamb
- pork
- veal
- wild boar

Nuts and Nut Butters

These can be eaten on their own (especially as snacks) or added to dishes to give them new flavors and textures. Some examples are:

- almond butter (natural, sugar-free)
- almonds
- Brazil nuts
- cashew butter
- cashews
- coconut butter
- hazelnut butter
- hazelnuts
- macadamia nuts
- walnuts

Poultry

Most children love fried chicken, so they'll be happy to know that they can continue eating this. Of course, chicken isn't your only option, in terms of poultry. Here are the best types of poultry to serve to your children:

- chicken (preferably free-range)
- goose
- quail
- turkey

Shellfish (preferably wild-caught)

Shellfish are rich in omega-3s, healthy fats, and other essential nutrients. You can cook them in many ways and there are plenty of options to choose from, including:

- clams
- crabs
- lobsters
- mussels
- oysters
- scallops
- shrimps

Sweeteners

Yes, you can still use sweeteners while cooking on Paleo. However, you must be very careful when choosing sweeteners, as there are only a few allowed on this diet. Some examples are:

- coconut sugar
- date sugar
- honey (raw)
- maple syrup

Vegetables

Vegetables are essential on this diet as they contain vitamins, minerals, and nutrients growing children need to stay healthy. Some of the best vegetables for children to eat on Paleo are:

- arugula
- asparagus
- beets
- bok choy
- broccoli
- Brussels sprouts
- cabbage
- carrots
- cauliflower
- celery
- cucumber
- kale
- mushrooms
- olives
- onions
- peppers
- pickles
- pumpkin seeds
- radish
- Romaine lettuce
- spinach
- squash

- zucchini

Beverages

It is important for children to stay hydrated so they don't get sick. Hydration is also essential for digestion. Here are the best beverages and liquids for children on the Paleo diet:

- bone broth
- coconut water
- sparkling water (with no artificial or natural sweeteners)
- water

While there are many types of food you can eat while on the Paleo diet, there are also those you should avoid. Knowing these foods will help you introduce this diet more effectively, especially if you want your children to follow it long-term. Here are the foods to limit or avoid while on Paleo:

Added Salt

While you can use small amounts of salt for your Paleo dishes, adding too much could easily cause a number of adverse health consequences, especially for children. While cooking on Paleo, it is recommended to taste your dishes throughout the process to ensure you aren't adding too much salt.

Dairy Products

Although dairy products aren't recommended, you may be a bit flexible with this, especially when it comes to your children. You can include cheese, butter, and full-fat milk. But you can also opt for non-dairy alternatives, especially for cooking.

Gluten and Grains

Gluten is considered an "anti-nutrient" and it's not suitable for the Paleo diet. Grains aren't recommended either. This means that you have to avoid pasta, bread, spelt, barley, rye, and other types of grain.

Highly-Processed Foods

Checking the labels of food products will help you determine if they are highly-processed. If they are, it's best to stay away.

Legumes and Nightshades

These foods are high in anti-nutrients that may cause different health issues. You can get the nutrients these foods contain from healthier sources like fish, meat, fruits, and vegetables.

Simple Sugars

Although children love sweets, simple or processed sugars

aren't allowed on the Paleo diet. Some examples of artificial sweeteners and other sweets to avoid are:

- acesulfame potassium
- aspartame
- candy
- cyclamates
- fruit juices
- ice cream
- pastries
- saccharin
- soft drinks
- sucralose
- table sugar

Some Types of Vegetable Oil

While you may use some types of vegetable oils, others aren't recommended simply because they are highly processed. Some examples of these are:

- corn oil
- cottonseed oil
- grapeseed oil
- safflower oil
- soybean oil
- sunflower oil

Trans Fats

You can find these in many different processed foods. If you spot the words "partially hydrogenated oils" or "hydrogenated oils," these are trans fats and it is best to avoid them.

When you eliminate several types of foods and food groups from your child's diet, you might be worried that they will develop nutrient deficiencies. This is why it's important to learn how to balance their meals and think carefully about the foods you serve them. If you are worried about nutrient deficiencies, speak with your child's doctor about your plans of starting them on the Paleo diet.

You and your child's doctor can come up with a plan to go about introducing the diet and having them follow it long-term. Your child's doctor can also monitor your child's health to make sure they are adjusting to the diet well and aren't experiencing any adverse effects. Your child's doctor might recommend a few modifications to your child's diet to make sure it is healthy and safe for them to follow.

WHY DOES THE PALEO DIET WORK?

When you consider the relative timespan we human beings existed on earth, the decades when our diets included processed grains and food is very short. Over thousands of years before this time, the bodies of our ancestors evolved to match their diet—the Paleo diet. Now, food is readily available to us. But in the past, our ancestors only ate what was available by hunting and foraging. Because of this, their physiology and metabolism became optimized for natural foods instead of the foods that are readily accessible to us now.

The Neolithic period wherein we discovered agriculture started around 10,000 years ago. Since then, we have refined our methods, and now, the processes of food production are very complex. But when you think about it, the time since we entered the Neolithic period until now only represents 1% of the total amount of time that human beings have roamed the earth. Proponents of the Paleo diet believe that our shift from a hunting-gathering diet to an agricultural one may have contributed greatly to the most common chronic health conditions of our day like diabetes, cardiovascular disease, and obesity. To avoid these issues, shifting back to the Paleo diet is key.

While this diet might seem too extreme for some, it actually makes a lot of sense when you understand why it works so well. Right now, our bodies are still genetically meant for a diet that focuses on whole, natural foods instead of processed ones. Since the Paleo diet is all about these natural foods, this makes it the ideal diet for us to follow.

But, as a parent, your next question might be: does this mean that it's good for children, too?

The answer to this question isn't definitive. But I will **vouch** that it has great potential to be very beneficial to its followers of all ages. As long as you know how to introduce the diet to your child properly, it can be an excellent dietary approach for the entire family. As your child continues to follow the diet, always make sure that whatever they eat is healthy and natural. Since whole foods are the main focus of this diet, this is another reason why it is beneficial for children.

These days, most kids eat lots of processed foods, both at home and in school. Since the Paleo diet discourages such foods, you will have to make a lot of changes to your child's diet. This is okay, of course, since these changes will ultimately make your child grow stronger and healthier. Biologically speaking, this diet is perfect for us. But when it comes to getting children to follow it, you must tread carefully. You don't want your children developing health issues because of this. At the end of the day, you want this diet to change your child's life for the better—and you can only do this by following the diet carefully and correctly.

WHAT ARE THE BENEFITS OF THIS DIET?

The benefits you and your children can enjoy on Paleo are similar to the benefits of eating healthy, whole foods. After all, this diet focuses on these types of foods. If you are already following this diet and you have been following it for some time now, then you ought to have started experiencing these benefits. If not, then you can look forward to the following positive effects:

Reduced Cravings

When you eat natural foods that your body needs, this has a positive effect on your cravings. While on Paleo, you will enjoy stable insulin levels throughout the day. This, in turn, helps reduce the cravings you feel. On Paleo, you will get all of the nutrients needed by your body without the addition of empty calories. The types of food you eat while on this diet help eliminate fluctuations in your energy levels. This doesn't just mean that your cravings will be reduced. It also means that you now stand the chance of consuming low-calorie foods that are rich in nutrients. This, in turn, helps you maintain a healthy weight.

This benefit is great for kids, too. After all, obesity is a major health issue with kids today. When you serve your child Paleo meals that mainly consist of healthy fats and lean protein, these will give your children a lot of energy while making them feel full for longer periods of time. Since Paleo is also relatively low-carb, your child's body starts learning how to use macronutrients effectively rather than relying mainly on glucose from carbs to provide energy. The carbs in this diet are complex carbs, which means that your child's body will utilize glucose more slowly. This prevents them from feeling hungry all the time and craving sugary, processed snacks.

Consistent Energy Levels

This benefit is related to the first one. While on Paleo, you will focus on foods that are low on the glycemic index. This means you won't have to deal with the energy drops that occur right after eating sugary foods or those high on the glycemic index. Learning how to plan your Paleo-friendly meals in the best way possible allows you to follow a well-balanced diet with all the macro and micronutrients required by your body. And the best part is, you will get these nutrients from whole, all-natural food sources.

As your children follow the same diet and eat the same healthy foods, it will make them feel more energized. By nature, children already have a lot of energy. But when they eat unhealthy, processed, and sugary foods, this causes them to experience spikes and crashes. Of course, it is still important to ask your child if they feel hungry because you have to make sure that they keep getting all of the nutrients needed throughout the day. For instance, even if your child isn't hungry, you can offer them a light but healthy snack if you feel like their caloric intake for the day is lacking. It's all about learning how to adjust your child's diet to meet their needs.

Anti-Inflammatory Effects

This benefit mainly comes from the fact that you will be cutting out processed foods from your diet. By nature, this diet encourages you to eat whole foods in their raw form as much as possible. This means you take in a lot of fruits, veggies, nuts, and seeds. For the rest of the foods like eggs, meat, and fish, for example, you would have to cook them first. Either way, these foods all have anti-inflammatory effects, an important benefit that helps prevent the development of various chronic diseases.

By eliminating grains and other foods prohibited on the Paleo diet, you will also be eliminating the anti-nutrients they contain. Even young children can enjoy this benefit. As they grow up, they won't have to deal with the cumulative effects of consuming inflammatory foods all their lives. This means that the Paleo diet greatly reduces their risk of developing chronic diseases later on in life. As your child grows up, they will enjoy a better quality of life thanks to the change in their diet that you started while they were young.

As simple as this might seem, your child will thank you when they're older.

Weight Loss

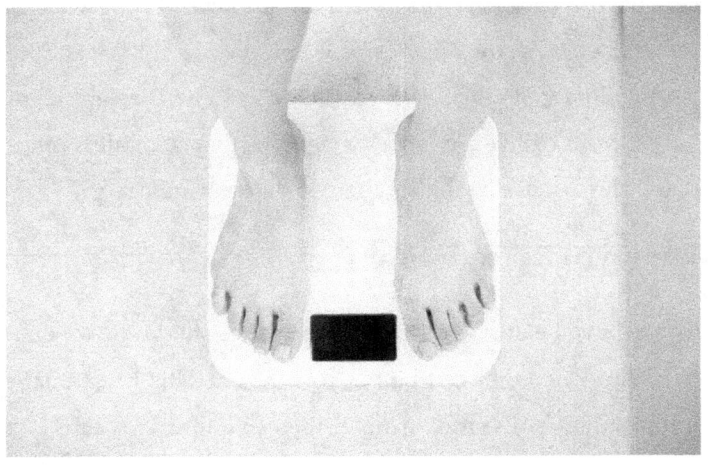

Fig. 3: Weight Loss. Unsplash, by i yunmai, 2018, https://unsplash.com/photos/5jctAMjz21A/ Copyright 2018 by i yunmai/Unsplash.

Since the core principle of the Paleo diet is the consumption of natural, unprocessed foods, and involves the consumption of limited carbs, it can definitely help you lose weight. Just make sure when you reach a healthy weight, you shift to maintain it instead of trying to lose more weight.

For children, this benefit is important if they are either overweight or obese. Children who are obese tend to grow up into adults who are obese if they don't lose weight while young. Also, according to a study, weight loss for obese children can help reverse insulin resistance (Zeybek et al., 2010). If your child already has a healthy weight, you should monitor their weight closely. You shouldn't allow your child to start losing weight, especially if they are neither obese nor overweight. Make sure your child eats enough each day and check their weight regularly. If your child experiences weight loss, make modifications to the diet to make it safer for them to follow it long-term.

Improved Heart Health

There have been several studies that have shown how beneficial the Paleo diet can be for your heart. This is especially important if you suffer from diabetes, as heart disease is a common complication associated with this condition. By following Paleo, your cholesterol levels may improve, too, as compared to other diets. Of course, this is also beneficial for children as it lowers their risk of developing heart diseases. This means when they grow up, they won't have to worry about this health issue much because the diet they are following is healthy for the heart.

Improved Insulin Resistance

Finally, the Paleo diet can also improve your insulin resistance. This is because your focus would be on eating foods that are generally low on the glycemic index. If you suffer from diabetes, you may want to ask your doctor about the possibility of following this one-of-a-kind diet. It can help you lose weight, improve your blood sugar levels, and make you feel better overall. Since the diet is also low-carb, your pancreas won't be under too much pressure to produce and release insulin all the time. This is another preventive benefit the Paleo diet offers to children. Improving their insulin resistance early on can help lower the risk of developing health issues related to insulin resistance.

Apart from all of these health benefits, another thing that makes this diet great is how realistic it is. Since you have lots of ranging options in terms of the foods to eat, you won't feel restricted. Although you may have to say goodbye to your favorite processed treats, you can simply find healthier, Paleo-friendly alternatives. The same thing goes for your children. Ease them into the diet so they don't feel like you're making drastic changes to their lives. As much as possible, try to make it a healthy and happy experience for them so they will be more willing to give this new eating approach a try.

2

ADAPTING PALEO FOR KIDS

Fig. 4: Paleo for Kids. Pixabay, by Luidmila Kot, 2020, https://pixabay.com/photos/baby-nature-vacation-food-tasty-5320542/ Copyright 2020 by Luidmila Kot/Pixabay.

At first glance, the Paleo diet might seem too restrictive, especially for children. But now that you know more about it, you may already have a better understanding of why a lot of people all over the world choose this diet to improve their health. When it comes to Paleo for kids, it's important to understand and accept that your aim here isn't necessarily to follow the diet perfectly.

As a parent, your main job is to structure a healthy Paleo-based diet that still allows your children to eat the foods they love. As long as you understand this, the Paleo diet can be totally safe for children. It offers a multitude of dietary options that are both delicious and filling. By introducing the Paleo diet to your child, you can explain the difference between unprocessed and processed foods. Part of introducing this diet is having a conversation with your child about the best types of food to fuel their body.

When it comes to the Paleo diet, it is best to introduce it to children at least 5 years old. By this time, they are already more efficient at eating solids and might even be more willing to try out different types of foods. When introducing a diet as unique as this to your child, it is best to do this in the least disruptive way possible. This means that you should start with familiar foods and work your way up. You don't want to introduce too many things too fast, as this might overwhelm your child, which, in turn, makes it more difficult to get them to follow the diet.

Adapting the Paleo diet to your child's life isn't just possible

—it can be quite easy, too. The key here is to learn how to tailor-fit the diet to your child's preferences and needs while trying to make little, gradual changes. In this chapter, we will talk about why you should put your kids on Paleo, the things to focus on when you're introducing this diet to them, and debunk the most common myths you might have heard. All of the topics discussed in this chapter will bring you closer to your goal of putting your child on this ancient diet. While there is still so much for you to learn, we will start with the simplest concepts to give you a better understanding of the "why" and "how" of following the Paleo diet with your children.

Why Should You Put Your Kids on Paleo?

Most of the studies and research on Paleo were conducted on adults. Of course, this makes a lot of sense because most parents don't put their children on specialized diets unless recommended by their child's doctor. Also, the studies are conducted on adults because this diet has the potential to combat chronic disease along with other healthy lifestyle changes. Since adults are more at risk for such diseases, health experts focus on them more.

However, because of the unhealthy foods that are readily available to children nowadays, young children have also become susceptible to developing these diseases. Take obesity, for instance. More and more children are suffering from obesity because they indulge too much in processed, sugary, and overall unhealthy foods. But aside from this common condition, children are now suffering from other chronic diseases like fatty liver disease and type 2 diabetes. One of the things the treatment of these diseases have in common is the consumption of healthy foods.

But there is still hope.

According to a study, the eating patterns and leisure time activities of school-aged children weren't healthy enough (Raynor et al., 2009). But early interventions at home, even as early as the preschool age, can help improve their eating patterns to improve their overall health, too. It is important to realize that the adverse effects adults see from eating junk and processed foods can also be experienced by children. In fact, since their bodies are still in the process of growing and developing, the effects might be more catastrophic.

While the Paleo diet isn't the "perfect" diet for children, it does have merit, especially if you modify it to suit your child's individual needs and preferences. The Paleo diet isn't just healthy and safe for kids, but it also has the potential to offer the following benefits:

Early nutrition has an impact on the development of your child's cognitive skills.

Good nutrition is important for young kids. The earlier you

start your children on good nutrition, the more you improve their health. In particular, early nutrition can help promote the healthy development of your child's cognitive skills. This is essential because children need these skills to learn other things throughout their lives.

Processed foods are harder to digest and they can have inflammatory effects on your child's body.

This benefit is especially important if your child suffers from any kind of food sensitivities. If you can eliminate the inflammatory foods from their diet, this will help improve their overall health. But even if your child doesn't have such sensitivities, this benefit makes it easier for them to digest their food, which, in turn, contributes to the healthy development of their digestive system. Beyond this, focusing on whole and natural foods can improve all other aspects of your child's health. So, if followed properly, the Paleo diet could make your child stronger and healthier overall.

The earliest development of chronic diseases can start in childhood—but this diet can help lower the risk.

These days, adults aren't the only ones at risk of developing chronic conditions. In fact, the earliest development of diabetes, cardiovascular disease, GI problems, and obesity can start in childhood. The Paleo diet is considered an early intervention. This dietary change helps lower your child's risk of developing these diseases along with other health benefits they can enjoy later in life.

Establishing healthy habits early makes them more permanent.

When you look back at the habits you have established early in childhood, they are often the most enduring ones. This means you still have these habits now that **you have reached adulthood.** Therefore, establishing healthy eating patterns while your child is still young and helping them understand the value of nutritious food at an early age helps ensure that they grow up with the things learned as children. This makes it easier for your child to continue eating healthily even when you're not around.

Your child will get the nutrients needed from the diet.

Even though you will be eliminating a number of foods from your child's diet, this doesn't mean they will miss out on essential nutrients. Since this diet focuses on healthy food sources, you will improve your child's diet in several ways. By encouraging your child to consume more nutrient-dense foods, you are also encouraging them to consume everything their bodies need to stay healthy each day. Of course, like any other diet, the key here is to find the right balance. And since you are introducing the diet to your child, you should also find ways to add variety so they always feel excited to eat the things you serve on their plates.

The great thing about the Paleo diet for kids is the variety of options to choose from. All you have to do is find the right balance while observing how the diet affects your child. Ideally, you can expect to see a lot of positive changes. But, just like other diets, this one does have a number of potential downsides that you should be aware of.

For one, your child might experience a number of symptoms like low energy, fatigue, or even changes in their digestion. Your child would be more at risk of these side effects if you try to make too many changes in their diet at once. Naturally, your child's body will adjust to the changes and they need time to get used to this new diet. To help avoid these common side effects, it is important to make sure your child is well hydrated. Making small changes is also effective, especially for younger children.

The development of nutrient deficiencies is another common issue your child might experience. However, you can easily avoid this by planning your child's meals well and by having regular checkups with your child's doctor, especially at the beginning. Once your child has adjusted to the diet, you will notice these potential downsides fade away. At the end of the day, it's your job as a parent to assess whether this diet is working for your child. Observation is essential, along with flexibility. And always remember that this diet isn't supposed to be perfect, especially when it comes to kids.

Try Not to Expect Perfection

If you want to make things easier for you, try not to think of Paleo as a strict diet to enforce on your child. Instead, think of it as a healthy lifestyle change that will improve your child's well-being. Since you will encourage your child to follow this diet, here are a few things to keep in mind:

Prepare yourself mentally for the task.

When you try to start following a diet, you need to be prepared for it. Now that you will be introducing the diet to another person—your child—it's important for you to set your mind to the task. This is going to be a long process that may involve challenges. As long as you remember why you are making this change in your child's life, you can motivate yourself and prepare yourself for what's to come.

Remember that this is about your child's health.

Your goals for following Paleo won't necessarily be your goals for introducing the diet to your child. At the end of the day, you should only focus on your child's health and safety. Always keep this in mind when you are making decisions or modifications in your child's diet.

Try not to expect perfection.

This is very important. Imagine how difficult it was for you to start the diet and stick with it. Expecting perfection from your child would be like setting them up for failure. Instead, it is better to simply "go with the flow" and allow things to happen. As long as you focus on what's important and keep observing your child, things will work out. Don't worry too much!

Keep things slow and simple.

If you really want your child to successfully adapt to the Paleo diet, it would be best to transition them into it gradually. For instance, you can start by introducing simple snacks to your child. After a week or two, start preparing one Paleo-friendly meal a day. This slow, steady, and simple approach makes it easier for your child to adjust to the diet, instead of trying to change all of their meals at once.

Also, it is important to remember that the younger your child is, the more flexible your approach must be. Use your best judgment when deciding when to serve Paleo meals or snacks to your child. Over time, you can start increasing the number of meals, but at the beginning, try not to rush things.

Be open-minded when choosing what foods to serve.

If you want your child to learn to love Paleo, you must learn how to be more open-minded, too. Sometimes, you might have to "break the rules" just so your child agrees to try out what you're serving them. In some cases, you might have to come up with a compromise. The good news is that things will become easier the longer you stick with your strategies. Soon, your children might start asking you to prepare the Paleo meals and snacks they find to be enjoyable and tasty.

Learn how to be realistic.

Right now, you don't have to be so focused on the details. While your child is still in the transition phase, you can still cater to their demands and cravings. Ultimately, you are in the process of crafting a version of the Paleo diet that best suits your child. Set small goals for your child and try to reach those goals without forcing them into anything. This lifestyle change takes time, and if you can accept that, you can learn to be more realistic with your expectations.

When you experience setbacks, keep going.

Yes, you will experience setbacks. These are normal and totally fine. The important thing is to learn from those experiences and keep going. If you discover that something isn't working, change it. If you find one of your strategies to be particularly effective, keep doing it. Introducing the Paleo diet to your child is a learning process for the both of you. Just keep moving forward and you're sure to find success.

Always remember that this process involves adjusting, too. Whatever you do, try not to be too harsh or forceful with your child. Take a gentle, positive approach and the whole experience will be more enjoyable for everyone involved.

FOCUS ON NUTRITION

The basic concept behind the Paleo diet is simple and healthy. But at the end of the day, you should focus on your child's nutrition. You should make sure your child is getting all of the nutrients needed to play, study, and grow. The Paleo diet differs from other types of diets as it doesn't depend so much on meeting specific macronutrient requirements.

For instance, if you were to follow the keto diet, you would have to greatly increase your fat intake, moderate your protein intake, and severely restrict your carb intake. Of course, such a breakdown wouldn't be ideal for growing kids. Since the Paleo diet primarily focuses on whole foods while limiting and avoiding processed foods, this makes it fairly flexible. If you want to make sure your child gets adequate nutrition from this diet, the best approach is to have a conversation with their pediatrician. Your child's doctor is the best person to give you advice about the nutritional needs of your child and how you can meet these while on Paleo.

As a parent, it is important for you to remember that the bodies of children are constantly growing and developing. This means their nutritional needs are vastly different from ours. Growing children need lots of vitamins, minerals, and fatty acids to support the development of their bones, the growth of their brains, and the overall maturation of their bodies. Aside from this, children are generally more active, which means they need adequate nutrition to fuel their bodies throughout the day.

Since the Paleo diet does eliminate certain foods and food groups from the diet, some parents are concerned that this also means you will be compromising your child's health, too. These concerns are valid, especially since they come from concerned parents. However, with the wide range of food options that are Paleo-approved, you don't have to worry about limiting your child's nutrient intake. The key here is to know which foods contain the nutrients they need —then make sure to include those foods in their daily diets. Here are some examples for you:

- To add calcium and fiber into your child's diet, feed them a lot of leafy, green veggies.
- To add complex carbs into your child's diet, feed them plantains and sweet potatoes.
- To add healthy fats into your child's diet, feed them salmon and avocado.
- To add protein into your child's diet, feed them eggs and lean meat.

In the previous chapter, we went through a comprehensive list of foods to eat while on Paleo. If you aren't sure about the vitamin, mineral, and nutrient content of certain foods, a simple online search will help you out. At the beginning of your child's Paleo journey, you will have to do a lot of research and planning to make sure you always feed them healthy and well-balanced meals. As time goes by, you will get used to these foods, which will make it easier for you to prepare your child's meals.

Introducing the Paleo diet to your child and encouraging them to follow it doesn't mean you have to follow it strictly. If you are on Paleo and you have completely eliminated all of the non-Paleo foods from your diet, good for you! But for children, there are a few considerations for you to keep in mind. This is especially true regarding the essential nutrients they need to grow and develop healthily. Some examples of these nutrients that children might not get enough of on Paleo are:

Calcium

This mineral is particularly essential to children (especially little girls) as they need it for the development of their bones. Since most dairy products aren't allowed on Paleo, this is one area where you can practice some flexibility. However, your children can also get this nutrient from dark green and leafy veggies, collard greens, and bone-in sardines or salmon. If you can incorporate these foods into your child's diet regularly, then you might not have to worry about them developing calcium deficiency.

Iron

Developing an iron deficiency can have a number of adverse health effects. Unfortunately, children who are either obese or overweight have a higher risk of being deficient in iron. Sometimes, though, even if your child is eating iron-rich foods, their body isn't absorbing or utilizing iron efficiently. In such a case, your doctor might recommend iron supplements for your child.

Vitamin D

While the best source of this vitamin is sunlight, you can add foods that are rich in vitamin D to your child's diet, too. While on Paleo, the best sources are salmon, mushrooms, egg (specifically the yolk), and sardines. Of course, it would also be ideal to allow your child to play outdoors as much as possible, as this has a lot of other benefits to their health and well-being.

You get the picture. As long as you are careful and conscious about your child's diet, you won't have to worry about compromising their nutrition. Just as you would plan your child's meals on any other kind of diet, focus on finding the right balance while trying to incorporate foods that they really enjoy.

FLEXIBILITY IS KEY

These days, more parents are becoming interested in the Paleo diet for themselves and their kids for the purpose of improving their health and wellness. At the very core, this diet is all about changing bad eating habits, like eating lots of sugary or processed foods instead **of** choosing healthier options.

Apart from focusing on whole, natural foods, another great thing about the Paleo diet is flexibility. Most diets—especially restrictive ones—aren't suitable for children. In fact, most diets are considered unsafe for children as they severely limit caloric intake. For others, they eliminate too many foods and food groups. This places children at risk of developing nutrient deficiencies. For these diets, you can barely make modifications, otherwise, they won't work as effectively.

By now, you already know that Paleo is different from these diets. On Paleo, you and your children have lots of options. Now, all you have to do is learn how to make the most of these options. Learn how to create winning dishes and meal plans to keep your children healthy, happy, and interested. When you and your kids switch to the Paleo diet (ideally, you would transition first), this can make your whole family healthier. Now that you understand the Paleo diet more, you may agree that feeding your child fewer processed foods and less sugar is a lot safer and healthier for their overall development and growth.

When encouraging your child to follow the Paleo diet, approach it in a clever and flexible way. For instance, it is not a good idea to immediately eliminate all sugary treats from your child's diet, especially if they are used to—and fond of—these foods. If you "forbid" your child from eating such foods, this will make those foods even more attractive to them. What's worse, your child might develop an obsession with sweets. As soon as you're not around (like if they're at school or as they grow older), they might gorge on sweets. Making drastic changes like this or being too strict with your child is counterproductive. Instead, you should try to go slow and keep the following things in mind:

Focus on establishing healthy nutrition at home first.

Since you are the one who prepares your child's meals at home, this is the best place for you to establish healthy nutrition. After you show your child that you are following Paleo and you're enjoying it, you can start introducing the diet to them gradually. Even if your child won't **keep to** this diet at school or when they attend parties, that's okay. As long as you consistently encourage your little one to develop healthy food habits at home, they will eventually have the same habits even outside of your home. Just remember that this is a process **with a long-term effect**.

Don't expect your child to follow Paleo all day, every day.

This is especially true at the beginning of your child's Paleo journey. Even if you end up introducing the diet at home, you don't have to force them to eat Paleo at every meal. Remember, being overly restrictive or forceful will cause your child to overindulge in the "forbidden foods" when they have access to these foods while you're not around.

Communicate openly with your child.

Once in a while, talk to your children about the Paleo-friendly foods you serve them. If they don't like some types of food, don't force them to eat those foods. Asking for their input also allows you to find out which foods they like. The more you communicate with your child about the diet you are encouraging them to follow, the more flexible you can be.

Paleo for kids takes a lot of careful thought and planning. In the beginning, you will have to do lots of trial-and-error as you learn how to go about the process. You will also learn more about your child as you observe them and talk to them about the changes you are making in their diet.

Even after your child has successfully transitioned into the Paleo diet, you still have to make plans if you want to maintain consistency. For instance, if you are attending a party with your kids, you can call the host beforehand and ask them about the food that will be served. If you discover that everything that will be served isn't Paleo-friendly, then you have to decide to either let your child eat at home before going to the party or allow them to indulge in non-Paleo foods while at the party.

To help you become more flexible, one thing you must remember is that there is no such thing as a perfect diet. All diets have their own advantages, disadvantages, benefits, and risks. Since you will be focusing on your child's diet, flexibility will help you succeed. Show your child that you are willing to accommodate their requests so that they will also be more willing to try the foods you serve them. It's all about making this a positive experience instead of a negative one.

DEBUNKING THE COMMON MYTHS

Fig. 6: Debunking Myths. Unsplash, by The Creative Exchange, 2020, https://unsplash.com/photos/UhpAf0ySwuk/ Copyright 2020 by The Creative Exchange/Unsplash.

Before we move on to the next chapter, where you will learn how to introduce the Paleo diet to your child and the rest of the family, let's debunk some of the most common myths that surround this diet. It will be very difficult for you to encourage your whole family to follow this diet with you if you still have doubts in your mind. So now, let's go through the common myths and concerns and also discover the truth behind them:

Your child won't get enough calcium

This myth comes from the fact that you will be cutting out dairy products from your child's diet. While this is true, this doesn't mean that you will be eliminating all food sources that contain calcium. The fact is, your children can get the calcium they need from green vegetables and other natural foods. Of course, since you will be following a modified version of this diet for your children (remember flexibility?), you may allow them to indulge in dairy products once in a while, especially during the transition period.

You have to completely eliminate carbs from your child's diet.

This is a very common myth that has absolutely no truth to it. Although the Paleo diet doesn't include food sources that are high in carbs, this doesn't mean you have to eliminate carbs altogether. Instead, you should get high-quality carbs from natural sources such as starchy vegetables and fruits instead of processed sources like cereals or bread.

Our hunter-gatherer ancestors had a shorter lifespan.

There might be some truth to this, but the shorter lifespan of our ancient ancestors wasn't caused by their diet. Most of them died from accidents, infectious diseases, and harsh environments. But when it comes to the food they ate, they followed a healthy diet that didn't cause the development of the modern-day diseases we have now.

If we take away the most common causes of our ancestors' deaths, they might have lived a lot longer. Of course, most of the foods that our hunter-gatherer ancestors ate aren't available now. So, we are actually following a modified version of this diet wherein we eat the healthiest alternatives to the foods **they consumed**. In following such a diet, we can improve our health in many ways. This, in turn, may improve longevity, too.

Going Paleo is too expensive.

This is one myth that might have been true in the past. When the Paleo diet was still "new," it would have been quite challenging to follow it, especially since it is vastly different from the traditional Western diet. But since Paleo has grown in popularity, the food industry has stepped up. Now, you can find so many Paleo-friendly food options that are healthy, tasty, and affordable, too. And if you choose to prepare your own meals using fresh, whole ingredients, this makes the diet even more economical!

Your child will consume excessive amounts of protein.

This is one concern that you shouldn't entirely ignore. There is such a thing as protein toxicity, a condition caused by the excessive consumption of protein. When you suffer from this condition, the health of your liver and kidneys is compromised. However, those who follow the Paleo diet correctly (which means that they make sure to balance their meals) never actually develop this condition.

Just because you are allowed to eat a lot of meat in this diet, it doesn't mean that you should only eat meat. This applies to your child, as well. Remember, you must find the right balance when it comes to planning your child's meals. In doing this, you don't have to worry about protein toxicity or any other associated health issues.

The diet lacks fiber.

Here's one myth that doesn't make a lot of sense. After all, fruits and veggies are encouraged on this diet. If you think that this is an issue, all you have to do is increase your intake (or your child's intake) of fiber-rich fruits like bananas, apples, and berries, as well as fiber-rich vegetables like carrots, broccoli, and artichokes. Nuts and seeds are high in fiber, too, so you can include these in your child's meals to boost their fiber intake.

We need whole grains to stay healthy.

For millions of years, our ancestors who lived in the Paleolithic era survived and thrived without consuming grains. This is because almost all of the food groups that are allowed in the Paleo diet already contain all of the vitamins, minerals, and nutrients our bodies need to stay healthy. In fact, grains don't offer enough nutritional value to compensate for the adverse side effects that you might experience when consuming too much of them.

Going Paleo long-term will lead to kidney damage.

You might be at an increased risk of developing kidney damage on a highly restrictive diet that only encourages the consumption of protein. Of course, you should already know by now that the Paleo diet isn't like this at all. Again, you can avoid this by balancing your child's meals and making sure that they get all of the nutrients they need each day. Also, you shouldn't restrict your child's diet drastically to avoid the risk of this health issue and other health issues, too.

The diet isn't nutritionally balanced.

Yes, the Paleo diet has the potential to be nutritionally unbalanced—if you don't follow it correctly. For instance, those who believe that the diet is all about meat just because it's also known as the "caveman diet" might only focus on eating meat at every meal. Naturally, this will lead to nutrient deficiencies. When this happens, such people will blame the diet for being all wrong for them.

But now that you understand this diet well and you know that you can control what you eat on it, you can plan your meals and the meals of your family to be tasty, healthy, and nutritionally balanced. It's all about being aware of what you are putting on your plates and what food combinations can boost your health.

Paleo doesn't offer variety.

Again, this is just not true! The Paleo diet offers a wide range of food options, and the more you learn how to prepare and cook your meals, the more variety you can have. Paleo-friendly ingredients are healthy, vibrant, fresh, and exciting. Later, we will go through a number of kid-friendly recipes you can start making right now. But don't stop there. A simple online search will give you a wide array of options to choose from and when you get the hang of cooking, going Paleo with your whole family becomes much, much easier.

There you have it—the most common Paleo-related myths and the truth behind them. As you can see, the Paleo diet isn't as "sinister" as some people think it is. Now, let's move on to the practical chapters of this eBook as you start learning how to introduce Paleo to your kids and how to start cooking Paleo-friendly meals for kids.

3

STRENGTH IN NUMBERS—BRINGING YOUR WHOLE FAMILY ON BOARD

Fig. 7: Paleo Family. Pixabay, by Виктория Бородинова, 2020, https://pixabay.com/photos/mom-mother-family-kids-picnic-5185568/ Copyright 2020 by Виктория Бородинова/Pixabay.

The key to permanently transitioning to the Paleo diet is to stick with it. The more united you are as a family, the more you increase your chances of succeeding in this diet. For instance, if you are the only one who follows Paleo while your partner is following the standard Western diet, it might be very challenging to convince your children to eat healthier food. Imagine how they would feel if your partner is having a plate of your children's favorite pasta while you are eating a vegetable dish. Even if that dish is tasty, your children will still resent the fact that they don't get to eat their favorite pasta, too.

On the other hand, if you and your partner are following the same diet, it becomes easier to encourage your kids to do the same. You won't have to prepare different dishes (which means it is a lot easier for you) and your children won't have to feel like you are restricting them from eating the foods they like. So, if you want your children to start following the Paleo diet, you may want to involve everyone else in your household, too—especially your partner.

When the household is fully involved, you can all make decisions together. You can plan meals together, share those meals, and enjoy all the benefits of the Paleo diet as you start experiencing them. For a lot of people, one of the main reasons they cannot sustain a diet is **the feeling of being** the only one in their home who follows the diet. This means they are constantly tempted with the foods they aren't supposed to eat no matter where they go. This makes them feel they are being too restricted and, in most cases, end up feeling miserable. Naturally, if you feel this way, you wouldn't want to follow the diet anymore. And when you decide to give up, you end up believing that it wasn't as effective to begin with.

In this chapter, we will focus on how you can encourage your whole family to start following this diet with you. While all of the tips you will learn here are meant to help you introduce the diet to your children, you can also use them to encourage other members of your household (specifically the other adults) to get on board, too. If you can do this, then they can even help you introduce the diet to your children.

As you all follow the diet together, you can all encourage each other to stick with it. Furthermore, you can take turns in planning your meals or making suggestions for new recipes to try. There is strength in numbers, and you will understand this when you unite your entire family to move toward the same goal. Explain to them the benefits of the diet and your plans for getting your kids on board. Just like you, the more they understand why Paleo is so effective, the greater the likelihood they will want to follow it, too.

STARTING SMALL

Recently, more families are transitioning to the Paleo diet for the purpose of improving their health and wellness. When people truly understand what the diet is all about, they understand why it works and why it will be beneficial for them—even for their kids. If you are already on the Paleo diet, you should know how effective it is.

But now, think back to when you started following the diet. The first thing you likely did was to learn more about the diet. This is an essential step because it allows you to determine whether or not you should follow the diet. In the same way, learning everything about Paleo, specifically Paleo for kids, allows you to make the right choice as a parent. After doing your research, what was the next thing you did?

Did you dive right into the diet, or make a plan for how to follow it first? Even if you succeeded in Paleo when you dived right into the diet without making a plan, this strategy isn't the best one if you want to introduce Paleo to your children. Think about it: to make sure your children are eating healthy meals every day, you plan those meals, right? Planning works, especially when it comes to new diets.

Also, planning allows you to introduce the Paleo diet in the best possible way—by starting slow. Since this diet is different from the diet your children are used to, making drastic changes isn't recommended. In fact, convincing your children to eat healthier foods might be one of the most challenging parts of being a parent. Since Paleo is all about healthy, whole foods, you need to make a plan of how to incorporate this new eating approach into their routines. To help you out, here are some steps you may follow when it comes to starting slow:

Choose one type of food to eliminate from your child's diet. Think about a food item that your child doesn't eat frequently anyway. For instance, eliminate sweet pastries, to start.

Check your kitchen and pantry to make sure that you don't have any of these sweet pastries stocked in your refrigerator or cabinets. After checking, make a mental note to stop purchasing this food item.

For a whole month, avoid feeding your child any kind of sweet pastry. If your child asks for a sweet pastry (like chocolate croissants or donuts), suggest a different type of food instead. You can give them a bowl of yogurt mixed with sweet berries, or a homemade dessert to satisfy their sweet tooth.

After a month, choose another type of food to eliminate from your child's diet. Then repeat the same steps as you did with the sweet pastries.

This is a simple and easy strategy to gradually wean your child off the unhealthy foods that aren't allowed on the Paleo diet. When your child has gotten used to Paleo-friendly foods (you should introduce these types of foods as a replacement for the ones you are eliminating), then you can eliminate more types of food at a time. Just remember to remain flexible and focus on your child's nutrition whilst introducing the diet to them slowly.

ALL ABOUT MEAL PLANNING

Fig. 8: Meal Planning. Pixabay, by Vegan Liftz, 2019, https://pixabay.com/photos/meal-plan-diet-plan-eating-healthy-4232109/ Copyright 2019 by Vegan Liftz/Pixabay.

As you follow the Paleo diet, gradually changing the foods your child eats at every meal might be a challenge, especially if they are used to seeing their plates filled with bread, pasta, dairy, and other non-Paleo foods. But since you won't be changing your child's diet drastically, this diet doesn't have to be too difficult to follow. In fact, it will make your child's diet simpler as you "go back to the basics" and focus more on natural foods. This means that your little ones would have to say goodbye to most junk foods like potato chips, fruit juices, ice cream, and sweets.

While you might feel excited at the prospect of improving your child's diet, it can also feel overwhelming. How do you go about this process? How do you make changes in your child's diet without making them feel restricted or resentful? How do you make sure your child successfully transitions into the Paleo diet? We have already discussed the most basic things to do in preparation for this transition. When it comes to introducing this diet and encouraging your child to follow it, one of the most helpful things you can do is to start meal planning.

Meal planning is a process that involves planning ahead for the meals to be cooked at home. In this case, you will be planning your child's meals—or, better yet, the meals for your whole family. While meal planning may take some getting used to, it can be very beneficial once you get the hang of it. Since meal planning is an effective method of introducing the Paleo diet and making sure you all stick with it, learning how to begin this process will help you out immensely. But before we go through some tips to help you start meal planning, let's discuss some of the most important benefits that meal planning has to offer:

It offers you flexibility.

Meal planning involves planning your own meals and the meals of your children. This means you get to customize the dishes at each meal, the ingredients you use to make those dishes, and even the macronutrient content of your dishes throughout the day, if you plan to count calories while on Paleo.

This means that you won't have to follow any standard diet plan—instead, you get to decide. Since flexibility is very important for this diet, especially when it comes to Paleo for kids, this is one benefit to look forward to when planning your meals.

It allows you to take a break from Paleo when you need to.

This is another excellent benefit you and your children stand to enjoy. Since you will be planning your meals (usually for a week), you can set days or meals when you and your kids take a break from Paleo. This can be very helpful, especially at the beginning of your child's transition.

For instance, if you are in the process of introducing Paleo, you can start by planning one Paleo meal a week. On Monday, you can have a Paleo breakfast, on Tuesday, you can have a Paleo snack, and so on. After three weeks or so, you can have two Paleo meals three to four times each week. This is an effective way for you to gradually introduce the diet. It also allows you to observe how your children react to the Paleo meals and whether or not they enjoy eating healthy, natural ingredients.

When your children have completely transitioned to the Paleo diet, you can also plan to take a break from it once in a while. For instance, if one of you is celebrating your birthday, you may choose to treat your children to a non-Paleo dessert like ice cream. Since you get to decide what meals you and your children have each day, you can make decisions as needed. You could also involve your children in the meal planning to empower them and make them feel happier about their new diet.

It saves time and money.

Finally, meal planning can save you a lot of money and time. For the former, the Paleo diet is all about whole, healthy foods. The good news is that these foods are usually cheaper than processed or junk foods. For the latter, once you get the hang of meal planning, it becomes routine for you. One day a week, you will be planning your meals, buying ingredients, preparing the ingredients you bought, and cooking your meals. Then, you get to store the meals you have prepared in the refrigerator.

For the rest of the week, all you have to do is reheat the meals and eat them! It's simple, easy, and it saves you a lot of time. This process also helps you make sure you always have Paleo-friendly meals at home in case your children are hungry.

If you can incorporate meal planning into your routine, you will realize what a life-saver it is. Now, if you want to start learning how meal planning works, here are a few tips to help you get started:

Decide what your meal planning routine will be.

For most people, meal planning is done once a week. Let me share my meal-planning routine. Since I work from Monday to Friday, I don't have time to plan our meals and cook them during these days. So, every Saturday morning, I sit down with my morning cup of coffee to plan our meals for a whole week. Since I have been meal planning for some time now, this task only takes around half an hour. But when I was starting out, I really struggled as it took me between one to two hours to complete our plan. As I kept practicing, I became faster at planning meals.

I shop for the ingredients I need every Saturday afternoon, usually after lunch. Then, for the whole Sunday morning, I prepare and cook all of our meals for the week. This is one example of what your meal planning routine might look like. You can use this example to create your routine or see what kind of schedule works well for you. It's all about finding what works and what makes things easier.

Choose the recipes to cook for the week.

The main part of meal planning is to choose the meals to cook. If you haven't been cooking in the past, then you will want to start with simple recipes. But if cooking is already part of your routine, you can choose between simple or complex recipes to whip up for your family.

During the transition period, think about which meals of the day you will set as Paleo. Then, you can gradually increase the frequency of your Paleo meals over time. Think about your children as you are planning meals. Since you want to introduce Paleo to your children, they have to be your priority. Make sure the meals you plan are healthy, interesting, and child-friendly.

Make your shopping lists.

As you plan your meals, it's helpful to have two additional sheets of paper beside you. This is where you get to write down the ingredients needed for your meals. It will be helpful to have a recipe book with you as you plan, unless you have memorized a couple of Paleo-friendly recipes already. This is one book that you can use while planning because it contains a lot of kid-friendly Paleo recipes for you to cook.

As you choose a recipe, write it down on your meal plan for the week. Then, write down all of the ingredients you need for it on one of the sheets of paper. When you're done with all of your plans, the next step is to check your pantry and refrigerator to see if you have any ingredients or prepared meals left over from last week. If you find any ingredients that are on the list you made, cross them out. Then, write down your final list of ingredients on the other blank sheet of paper. This is the list you'll **be** taking down to the supermarket.

Involve your children in the process.

To make your children's transition easier, involve them in your meal planning. Do this after a few weeks of following the Paleo diet so that your children are already familiar with the diet and the foods they should be eating. Then, you can ask them to help you plan the meals. Allow them to choose one Paleo meal, one non-Paleo meal (or snack), and one Paleo meal you get to cook together. This level of involvement makes meal planning more fun for you and your children. It also encourages them to feel more interested in the diet because they will look forward to planning and cooking dishes with you.

Learn to love cooking.

Since cooking is the other side of meal planning, it's important for you to learn to love cooking, too. If you haven't cooked much in the past, you should know that it becomes easier for you to go Paleo if you cook your meals from home. You can choose the ingredients to use, the dishes to make, and how to cook them. The more you practice cooking, the easier it becomes. For a lot of people (including me), cooking is a calming activity. Then, you will master the art of meal planning.

When you have learned to love cooking, you can involve your children in this process, too. Cooking with kids can be very enjoyable, and this is one skill that can benefit children in different ways. Allow your children to help you cook simple, Paleo-friendly recipes. This is another way to make it easier and more enjoyable for them to transition into this unique, and healthy diet that our ancestors followed.

Unleash your creativity.

Once you get the hang of meal planning, you can start being more creative with it. Occasionally, have "themed days" like Taco Tuesday or Pizza Friday. Since the Paleo diet includes a wide range of foods, you can create virtually any kind of dish that will be suitable for the diet. Although you can unleash your creativity through meal planning, you can also invite your children to unleash their creativity, too. Come together and think about fun themes to make your process of meal planning more motivational. And when those themed days come, involve your children in the cooking process.

Include leftovers in your meal plans.

Although meal planning allows you to prepare all of your meals for the week, this doesn't necessarily mean that you will be able to eat all of the meals you have prepared. In some cases, you might end up having leftovers, either because you prepared too much food or you and your family didn't eat at home at some point during the week. In any case, you shouldn't throw out your leftovers. Instead, include them in your meal plans for the next week. Have these leftovers first, then eat the other dishes you have prepared in the following weeks.

Keep practicing!

Just like any other skill, meal planning needs to be practiced. The more you plan your meals, the easier this process becomes. Try to be as consistent as possible when meal planning. For instance, plan your meals at the same time and the same day each week. This consistency will make it part of your routine. But if you feel like there is something that isn't working in your process, modify it.

Meal planning should suit your needs and lifestyle. You

shouldn't have to change your life just to follow other people's meal-planning routines. You have to enjoy this process for it to be sustainable—and the best way to do this is by tweaking your process until you're happy with it. Then, as you continue doing it, you get better at it.

AS A PARENT, WHAT'S YOUR ATTITUDE TOWARD FOOD?

If you're currently on the Paleo diet, can you remember your reasons for starting the diet in the first place? Most people want to lose weight, focus more on whole, natural foods, or take necessary steps to improve their health. No matter your reasons for going Paleo, if you want this to be your permanent approach, then you should consider it a lifestyle change instead of simply following a diet.

As an adult, it is easy for you to label certain foods as "bad" or "restricted." You understand that these foods aren't recommended on Paleo, so it is best to avoid them. But the methods you use to motivate yourself to stick with the diet might have adverse effects on your children—the most common of which is the development of eating disorders.

When it comes to introducing a diet, your attitude about it is extremely important. If you try Paleo and you feel it doesn't work, you shouldn't try introducing it to your children. But if you have started the diet and you are already experiencing all of the benefits, you will feel more enthusiastic about it. This kind of situation is ideal because your enthusiasm will rub off on your kids. Also, the more you know about the diet (because you are following it), the more practical and effective strategies you have when introducing the Paleo diet to your children and inspire them to stick with it.

Do you still remember the diet you used to follow when you were young? Unless your parents were very focused on nutrition, chances are, they probably didn't put you on any diet. But these days, due to the risks of chronic diseases, parents like you and me are more interested in trying to reduce our children's intake of unhealthy, processed, and junk foods. So, here you are, learning all about the Paleo diet and how to apply it to your children. As a parent, you should try to adopt a positive attitude toward food—not just the Paleo diet, but toward food in general.

It is important for you to show your children the value of healthy food and why you want to focus on natural foods instead of the convenient, ready-made, packaged ones. Changing your mindset toward food and adopting a positive attitude will inspire the same changes in your kids. This way, instead of feeling like you are restricting them, they get to understand that it is important to seek healthier food options to nourish their bodies and keep them healthy. Although this is a very abstract concept, you can teach it to your children by showing them positivity instead of trying to explain it to them. When you see positive changes in your children, then you can take things further by doing the following:

Have a conversation about food, nutrition, and the Paleo diet.

After you consistently show a positive attitude toward healthy food to your children, try to observe if they are mimicking you. If you see that your child is starting to make healthier food choices—like if you offer your child a choice between a piece of chocolate and a piece of fruit for a snack, and they choose the fruit—this is the perfect time to have a positive and enriching conversation with them about food, nutrition, and the Paleo diet.

Talk about the difference between processed foods, whole foods, and how these foods affect our health. The language you use when explaining these things should be age-appropriate. For instance, you have to use simple words when talking to a four-year-old, but you can use more technical terms when talking to a nine-year-old. This is the first thing you should explain, because it is fairly simple.

A few days later, start a conversation about healthy food

habits. Review the concepts your child has learned about processed and whole foods, then use this to introduce healthy eating habits to them. Here, you can ask them questions about whether or not they are already following these healthy food habits. Then you can talk to your child about how these healthy food habits can make them grow big and strong.

Finally, after some discussions about food and nutrition, you can introduce the basic principles of the Paleo diet. Talk to your child about the simplicity of the Paleo diet and why you would like them to follow it. Since you have already shared previous discussions, your child will have a more nuanced understanding of why the Paleo diet is beneficial to their health. Just remember to show honesty and enthusiasm when talking about these things with your children. Try not to sound pushy or bossy. In fact, if you can explain these things through games or stories, that would be even better! Be as creative as possible so that your child sees that you just want to change their diet to improve their health.

Avoid using black and white terms when talking about food

Whenever you talk about food, try to avoid using definitive labels. For instance, saying that some foods are "good" while other foods are "bad" makes children feel more interested in the "bad" options. Go back to flexibility. Remember that you will not restrict your child while on this diet, so labeling things this way will be counterproductive to your goals. Instead, you should try the approach of sharing the benefits of healthy, Paleo-friendly foods while telling them that there are some types of food they may have to stay away from because they aren't good for their health.

You can even say that you aren't going to prevent them from eating such foods. If your child wants to eat candy, for instance, allow them to. Tell your child that they are welcome to eat candy, but not too much because of the adverse health effects they might experience as a result. The next time they ask for the same unhealthy food, try offering a healthier alternative. Then remind them that the food you are offering is healthy and it tastes just as sweet as candy. The point here is to try your best to emphasize the benefits of Paleo-friendly foods while gradually trying to phase out the ones that aren't Paleo-approved without making it seem too obvious.

Share your experiences about following the Paleo diet.

For this tip, you can only do it if you have been following the Paleo diet before introducing it to your child. This is why it is ideal to experience the diet yourself, first—so you can share your experiences with your child. Talk about your favorite Paleo meals, your favorite Paleo snacks, and how it felt when you replaced non-Paleo foods with healthier alternatives. Also, talk about how following this diet made you feel better, stronger, and healthier.

You can even share experiences to help them understand the adverse effects of processed foods. For instance, if you have ever gotten sick from eating too much junk food, tell your children about it. Try to be honest about your experiences. Children have a way of knowing if you are telling the truth. Also, sharing real experiences shows your child that you really believe in this diet and that you have a very positive perspective about it.

If you have a positive attitude toward the Paleo diet, you will also have an easier time following it. Then, you can think of creative ways to get your children on board. For instance, why don't you try cooking your child's favorite dish with a twist? Analyze the recipe and see which ingredients are non-Paleo. Then, go online and do your research. Find the best Paleo-friendly alternatives for those ingredients. Try to cook the dish using those ingredients and see if it tastes the same. Sometimes, the dish will taste even better!

Your attitude about healthy eating habits plays an important role in how well your children will adopt the same habits. Try to make their transition as positive as possible. Help your children understand that this diet can change their life in wonderful ways. Then, as you transition together as a family, mealtimes in your home become easy, breezy, and healthy. If your partner and the other adults in your household can show the same positivity, that would be even better!

The great thing about this is that your children will continue to follow the Paleo diet even when you're not around. For instance, if there is a party at school where food is served, your children might make a conscious choice to select foods that are allowed on their diet. This is when you know that your child has become used to the diet, as they would still follow it even if they are presented with other options. Of course, at this point, you still have quite a long way to go.

LEADING BY EXAMPLE

As a parent, you have a very strong influence on the actions and the choices of your children. You might have noticed this already: they copy what you do, imitate the things you say, and even try to dress like you. This is because you are the most important person in your child's life and they want to be just like you. Now that you know this fact, you can take advantage of it by setting good examples for your children, especially when it comes to the Paleo diet. Here are some tips to help make your child's Paleo journey easier as you lead by example:

Encourage positivity toward food and nutrition.

Show your children that you are excited about the change they are about to embark on. Tell them how much your life has improved because you started following the Paleo diet and now, you want their lives to improve, too. Even on days when you are craving something sweet, starchy, and generally non-Paleo, try not to let these feelings show. You may express them to your partner (who, ideally, is also on Paleo) but not to your children. When it comes to your kids, focus on showing positivity toward food, nutrition, and healthy eating habits.

Avoid demonstrating bad or unhealthy habits, especially while your child is around.

As adults, we sometimes have unhealthy or bad habits that we cannot seem to get rid of. While it would be better for you to try and eliminate these bad habits, if you can't, just make sure you aren't demonstrating them when your children are around. For instance, there are some alcoholic beverages that aren't recommended on Paleo, such as beer and sugary cocktails. Drinking these in front of your kids isn't ideal. First, because alcohol consumption is generally considered a bad habit, especially when you drink excessively. Second, such beverages aren't recommended on Paleo.

Another example of an unhealthy habit you should never demonstrate in front of your children is binge eating. When you are transitioning into the Paleo diet, you might have moments when you just can't resist your cravings. So, you might allow yourself to binge on non-Paleo foods just to give in to these cravings. If your children see you doing this, however, they might think that binge eating is okay. These are just some examples of things you should try to eliminate from your life. But, if you can't, just don't do them in front of your children.

Avoid using food as punishment or reward.

This is a common mistake that a lot of parents do without even realizing they're doing it. For instance, if your child does something bad, you "punish" them by forcing them to eat their veggies. Unfortunately, this will make your child associate veggies with bad feelings. Whenever you try to encourage them to eat veggies (which are very important on Paleo), they suddenly feel like you're punishing them. In the same way, if your child does something nice and you "reward" them with a sweet treat, they will associate these foods with good feelings. This makes it very difficult to wean your child off such foods. Avoid using food this way. Instead, emphasize the importance of food in our lives, especially the importance of Paleo-friendly foods to our health and well-being.

Encourage your children to prepare or cook food with you.

A very effective way to encourage children to become more adventurous with foods is by involving them in the preparation and cooking. Once in a while, invite your children to prepare the ingredients you intend to use for cooking. If they want to help you cook, too, allow them to. Cooking is an important activity that teaches important life skills to children. Aside from this, it also makes them feel like they are an active decision-maker when it comes to food. This increases their willingness to try new foods and eat the dishes that you have prepared together.

Show or express your appreciation of your child's effort to follow the Paleo diet.

As time goes by, your child will gradually get used to the Paleo diet. Whenever you see changes in this direction, express your appreciation. For instance, if your child asks you for a snack and you say, "What kind of snack?" and they choose one of the Paleo-friendly snacks you serve them, praise your child for this choice. Or, when you serve a Paleo meal and your child finishes everything on their plate, congratulate them for it. When your child sees that their actions are making you happy, there is a higher likelihood that they will continue doing those actions to please you.

Allow them to make decisions once in a while.

You can't expect to monitor your child's diet forever. At some point, they will have to start making their own decisions in terms of the foods they eat. You can practice this by allowing your children to make decisions about their food once in a while. This is why it's recommended to involve your children in meal planning. Allowing them to choose the meals they eat along with the whole family gives them a sense of empowerment.

Now, if you allow your child to decide and they choose a non-Paleo option, don't scold them for it. Accept their decision and continue encouraging them to follow the Paleo diet. Eventually, they will choose Paleo, just like you. If you notice that your child is constantly choosing non-Paleo options, you can encourage Paleo by allowing them to choose between two Paleo snacks or meal options. By doing this, you are still allowing them to make a choice, but this time, you have narrowed down their options so that whatever choice they make will be a step toward your long-term goals.

Show your child that you will always choose Paleo no matter where you are or what the situation is.

Speaking of choices, when *you* are faced with choices between Paleo and non-Paleo options, always choose the former—especially if your child is watching. Happily select veggies, fruits, and other whole foods over processed, sugary or junk foods each and every time. When your child sees that you constantly choose Paleo options, they might start doing this, too. When this happens, praise them for it and show them that you're happy with the choice they made.

Invite your child to learn with you.

Finally, when you need to do more research (like when you need to find Paleo-friendly recipes), invite your child to help you. You can do an online search to find recipes and, while you are looking at different options, ask for your child's input. For instance, if you're choosing between two breakfast recipes, see which one your child prefers. Exposing your child to this kind of activity makes them feel more interested in the Paleo diet altogether. Soon, your child might even ask you when your next research session will be!

When leading by example, try to focus on being a good role model. Always remember that children are constantly observing you. If they see bad habits, expect to see them doing the same. If they see healthy, Paleo-friendly habits, however, you can look forward to your children following your lead. As a parent, you have a very powerful role to play... so use your powers well!

4

LUNCH IS SERVED!

Fig. 9: Lunch. Unsplash, by Louis Hansel, 2020, https://unsplash.com/photos/bPNvATD1cvc/ Copyright 2020 by Louis Hansel/Unsplash.

Now that you know the basics of Paleo for kids, it is time to start cooking. As you have learned, one of the easiest ways to ensure that your children are following this diet closely is by making their meals for them. Here, I will share with you twenty different Paleo recipes that your kids—and the rest of your family—will love. We will start the chapter off with some Paleo ingredient shopping tips, then we will move on to the recipes. Most of the recipes shared here take half an hour or less to prepare, but a few of them take more time. Even as a beginner, you can easily follow these recipes, and as your skills increase, you can start aiming for more complex recipes to keep your children interested.

SHOPPING ON PALEO

While you and your kids are following the Paleo diet, you have to start making changes to your shopping list. This is especially true if you plan to cook your children's meals at home. When cooking for the Paleo diet, there are certain staples you have to stock up on. Apart from these, there are other foods you would have to buy to make sure your kids and the rest of your family eat meals and snacks that are suitable for this unique diet.

Here is a sample shopping list for you. It is a comprehensive list, but when making yours, you can simply pick out the things you need and write those down on a piece of paper to take with you to the supermarket. Here are some of the most common food items to buy for the Paleo diet:

Condiments

These add flavor to your children's meals and snacks. Although you want to avoid processed condiments, there are many options for you to choose from, such as:

Coconut aminos: This is a savory condiment you can use for marinades, salad dressings, and stir-fried dishes.

Coconut milk or cream: This condiment adds richness to smoothies, curries, and soups. It is also commonly used in baking.

Fish sauce: This condiment adds an umami flavor and some saltiness to soups, stews, salad dressings, and Asian-inspired dishes.

Mustard: There are several types of mustard you can use. Just check the labels to see if they're Paleo-friendly.

Tahini: This is a sesame seed paste with a smoky flavor that is commonly used in sauces, dips, and salad dressings.

Tamari: This is another soy sauce alternative (like coconut aminos) that is wheat- and gluten-free.

Vinegar: You can opt for balsamic or apple cider vinegar to use for cooking.

Eggs

The best option is the organic, free-range variety. These are nutrient-dense and the chickens that laid these eggs weren't injected with growth hormones or other harmful chemicals.

Fats and Oils

When using fats and oils for cooking on Paleo, there are a few ideal options, such as:

- coconut oil
- olive oil
- organic ghee

Fish and Seafood

Fish and seafood are excellent sources of protein and other nutrients on the Paleo diet. If your kids love seafood, then you may want to learn how to cook a number of dishes that feature these healthy food items. Some of the best options on Paleo are shrimp and wild-caught Alaskan salmon. Of course, other types of fish and seafood are great, too.

Fruits

Fruits are healthy and sweet, and there are lots of options to choose from. You can use fruits for cooking dishes or simply give them to your kids as a healthy snack instead of serving them something processed. Here are some examples of the most popular fruits that children love:

- apples
- bananas
- beets
- berries
- melons
- oranges
- tomatoes

Herbs and Spices

To make your dishes healthier and more flavorful, try adding herbs and spices. The more you experiment with these, you will learn which herbs go well with certain dishes and which spices improve the taste of others. Learning how to cook is a great experience for the whole family. Some Paleo-friendly options are:

- basil
- cinnamon
- cumin
- garlic powder

- ground flaxseed
- turmeric

Meat

When choosing meat, opt for organic, grass-fed varieties. This can include pork, beef, lamb, and other meat sources that your children will like. Once in a while, you could include more uncommon options like liver and other organ meats as these are very nutritious, too.

Nuts and Seeds

These food items are healthy, Paleo-friendly, and very versatile. They can be eaten as a snack or added to dishes to add texture and flavor.

Poultry

Just like other meat sources, it's better to opt for organic, free-range varieties when it comes to poultry like chicken, duck, or turkey. Such food products offer a higher-quality protein to make sure your kids are only eating the best.

Sweeteners

Just because your kids are on Paleo doesn't mean they can't have anything sweet. There are natural sweeteners like coconut sugar, maple syrup, and coconut syrup that can be used for cooking, especially when whipping up desserts or sweet snacks for your little ones.

Vegetables

Finally, veggies are an important part of any diet, especially Paleo. When it comes to veggies, there are few limitations. In fact, you should try to think of different dishes that incorporate vegetables as these contain a lot of vitamins, minerals, and nutrients that children need to grow healthy and strong. For instance, you can include the following veggies on your shopping list:

- asparagus
- broccoli
- Brussels sprouts
- carrots
- celery
- cucumber
- kale
- spinach

Cooking on Paleo—even for kids—doesn't have to be a scary or challenging thing. As long as you know what foods are suitable and you have a collection of simple recipes, you can easily maintain consistency with your children's diets. To help you start with your homemade meals, here are some easy, quick, and healthy recipes for you.

CRISPY BACON-WRAPPED CHICKEN

This easy recipe is a one-pan dish where you use chicken as the main protein. As simple as it might seem, it is packed with a lot of flavors. The tender chicken thighs are wrapped with crispy bacon that your children will love munching on. It is healthy, comforting, super filling, and you can add a side of potatoes or veggies to complete the meal.

Serving Size: 5 servings

Time: 20 minutes

Prep Time: 5 minutes

Cook Time: 15 minutes

Ingredients:

- ½ tsp sea salt (fine grain)
- ½ tsp smoked paprika
- 1 tsp olive oil
- 2 tsp onion powder
- 5 chicken thighs (boneless, skinless, cut in half)
- 10 slices of bacon

- black pepper

Directions:

In a bowl, combine the paprika, salt, pepper, and onion powder, then mix well.

Season the chicken thighs with the mixture, making sure that all of them are well coated.

Wrap a slice of bacon all around each of the chicken thigh halves. Try to cover all of the chicken thigh halves as much as possible with the bacon slices.

In an oven-safe skillet, add the olive oil over medium-high heat. Also, preheat your oven to 400 F.

Add each of the wrapped chicken thighs to the skillet and cook for about 2 minutes.

Turn the wrapped chicken thighs carefully to cook the other side for another 2 minutes.

Place the skillet into your oven and bake the wrapped chicken thighs for 10 to 15 minutes, until the bacon is crispy and the chicken thighs are cooked through.

Serve while hot with a side dish of choice.

CLASSIC MAC AND CHEESE

When it comes to pasta for kids, mac and cheese is a classic. Although this dish places a Paleo twist on the classic favorite, your kids might not even know the difference! It has a lovely sauce and it also includes vegetables. This recipe is a sneaky way for you to incorporate more veggies into your children's diets. Keep the ingredients to this recipe on hand, as your children might ask you to make it over and over again!

Serving Size: 4 servings

Time: 30 minutes

Prep Time: 10 minutes

Cook Time: 20 minutes

Ingredients for the mac:

- ½ tsp salt
- 2 tbsp butter (you can also use coconut oil)
- ½ cup of water
- 1 ½ heads of cauliflower

Ingredients for the cheese:

- ½ tsp garlic powder
- ¾ tsp ground mustard
- 1 tsp salt
- 2 tbsp butter
- 1 ½ cups of coconut milk
- ½ sweet onion (minced)
- 1 egg (yolk only)
- 1 small carrot (peeled, diced)
- 1 small summer or butternut squash (cut into small cubes)
- black pepper

Directions:

For the cauliflower, you have two options to choose from. First, cut off the leaves and stalks, then break it into pieces.

Add the broken-down pieces to an Instant Pot, along with a cup of water.

Adjust the settings of the Instant Pot to steam the cauliflower pieces for about 6 minutes.

For the second option, add the broken down pieces to a sauté pan, along with the rest of the mac ingredients, over medium-high heat.

Cover the sauté pan and allow the cauliflower to steam for

about 5 minutes. Make sure to check the level of water once in a while to ensure it doesn't dry out.

When the cauliflower is almost tender, set the lid aside and sauté for about 2 minutes to caramelize lightly.

Turn off the heat, put the lid back on, and start preparing the sauce.

In a saucepan, melt the butter over medium-high heat.

Add the carrot, onion, squash, salt, pepper, garlic powder, and mustard, and sauté the veggies for about 5 minutes until the onion has become translucent.

Add the coconut milk, mix well, and bring to a simmer.

Allow the mixture to simmer for about 10 minutes, until the coconut milk reduces and the vegetables have become tender.

Pour the mixture into a blender and pulse until you achieve a smooth consistency.

Add the egg yolk, then continue pulsing until fully incorporated. Since the mixture is hot, it will cook the yolk while thickening the mixture and making it richer.

Taste the sauce and add salt and pepper according to your taste.

Pour the sauce over the warm cauliflower and toss until fully coated.

Serve while warm.

PIZZA SOUP

Fig. 10: Pizza Soup. Pixabay, by Vicki McCarty, 2014, https:// pixabay.com/photos/chili-con-carne-chili-recipe-448364/ Copyright 2014 by Vicki McCarty/Pixabay.

Have you ever tried feeding your children pizza, but in the form of soup? Traditional pizza crust may not fit into the Paleo diet, but you can still let your children enjoy the flavors of pizza in a new and tasty way. This is a customizable recipe as you can add, remove, or replace the ingredients as you and your children prefer. It's quick, healthy, and it is sure to be one of your children's favorites.

Serving Size: 2 servings

Time: 30 minutes

Prep Time: 5 minutes

Cook Time: 25 minutes

Ingredients:

- 1 tsp garlic powder
- 1 tbsp oregano (dried)
- 2 cups of fire-roasted tomatoes (canned)
- 3 cups of button mushrooms (sliced)
- 3 cups of marinara sauce
- ¼ lb pepperoni (thinly sliced, preferably uncured)
- ¾ lb chicken sausage (thinly sliced)
- 1 large onion (diced)
- black pepper
- salt
- ¾ cup of olives (optional, sliced)

Directions:

In a saucepan, combine all of the ingredients.

Cook the pizza soup mixture for about 25 to 30 minutes, until the mushrooms and onions have softened.

As you are cooking, taste the pizza soup and add seasoning according to your taste.

Serve hot with a side of Paleo-friendly crackers. If you have any leftover pizza soup, you can store it in the refrigerator for 3 to 5 days. Then all you have to do is reheat the soup a few minutes before your mealtime. So simple!

COLORFUL VEGGIE TACOS

Instead of using taco shells, which aren't suitable for Paleo, you make use of crunchy collard greens! This makes the tacos healthier, fresher, and perfect for your children's new diet. These colorful vegetable tacos are super scrumptious and they will encourage your kids to eat more greens.

Serving Size: 6 tacos

Time: 30 minutes

Prep Time: 10 minutes

Cook Time: 20 minutes

Ingredients for the tacos:

- 1 tsp cumin (ground)
- 1 tsp onion powder
- 3 tbsp olive oil (divided)
- 2 cups of portobello mushrooms
- ¼ cup of harissa paste (optional, use a mild harissa paste to add spice)
- 6 leaves of collard greens
- cashew cream (optional, for topping)
- cilantro (optional, fresh, chopped, for topping)
- tomatoes (optional, chopped, for topping)

Ingredients for the guacamole:

- 1 tbsp cilantro (fresh, chopped)
- 2 tbsp lemon juice (freshly squeezed)
- 2 tbsp red onions (chopped)
- 2 tbsp tomatoes (chopped)
- 2 avocados (ripe)

salt

Directions:

Take the stems out of the portobello mushrooms.

Rinse the mushrooms, then pat dry with a paper towel.

In a bowl, combine 1 ½ tablespoons of the olive oil with the onion powder, cumin, and harissa, if desired. Mix well.

Brush each of the portobello mushrooms with the seasoning mixture. Make sure that the mushrooms are fully coated.

Allow the mushrooms to marinate for at least 15 minutes.

In the meantime, prepare the guacamole. Cut the avocados in half, remove the pits, and scoop the flesh out.

Mash the avocados, add the rest of the guacamole ingredients, and mix well. Set the guacamole aside.

Rinse the leaves of the collard greens, chop the tough stems off, and place on a plate.

In a skillet, add the rest of the olive oil over medium-high heat.

Add the marinated Portobello mushrooms to the skillet and cook one side for about 3 minutes.

Flip the mushrooms over and continue cooking for another 3 minutes.

Turn the heat off and allow the mushrooms to rest for about 3 minutes before you start slicing.

After resting, slice the portobello mushrooms into strips.

Start assembling your vegetable tacos. In each collard green leaf, add a couple of mushroom slices. Top with the guacamole and any other toppings you want to add.

Serve immediately with some kind of fried or grilled protein source, like fish or chicken.

FISHY SHEET PAN LUNCH

Sheet pan lunches are so simple and easy that these can be your go-to recipes when you don't have a lot of time to prepare complex dishes for your children. This particular recipe includes fish and different kinds of vegetables. It's another great way to add veggies to your children's diets, as the roasted veggies have a unique flavor that they will surely enjoy.

Serving Size: 4 servings

Time: 30 minutes

Prep Time: 5 minutes

Cook Time: 25 minutes

Ingredients:

- 1 ½ lb of salmon fillets (sliced or whole)
- 1 ½ cups of cherry tomatoes

- 1 large fennel bulb (slice it lengthwise to have "steaks")
- 1 zucchini (thinly sliced)
- 2 lemons (cut in half)
- black pepper
- kosher salt
- olive oil

Directions:

Preheat your oven to 450 F.

In a sheet pan, add the cherry tomatoes, fennel bulb steaks, and zucchini.

Sprinkle them with salt and pepper and drizzle with olive oil.

Toss all of the ingredients together until everything is fully coated. If needed, add more olive oil, salt, and pepper.

Arrange the ingredients around the sheet pan so that there is only one layer.

Place the sheet pan in the oven and bake the veggies for about 10 minutes.

Take the sheet pan out of the oven and push the veggies to one side.

Sprinkle salt and pepper over the salmon fillets, then place them on the sheet pan next to the veggies.

Place the sheet pan back in the oven and continue baking for 12 to 15 more minutes. The time you cook the salmon fillets will depend on their thickness and size.

Take the baking sheet out of the oven. Carefully transfer the veggies and salmon fillets to serving plates, and serve immediately with one lemon half each for squeezing.

HEALTHY CHICKEN BOWL

This healthy bowl is simple, hearty, and highly customizable. If you want to nourish your children with only the best ingredients, here's an excellent way to do it. You can even ask your children to help you with this recipe, as it is super easy and quick to do. It is a bowl of fresh goodness that you can prepare in half an hour. Perfect!

Serving Size: 2 servings

Time: 30 minutes

Prep Time: 5 minutes

Cook Time: 25 minutes

Ingredients:

- 1 tbsp avocado oil (you can also use olive oil)
- 1 ½ cups of roasted peppers (canned, drained)
- 2 cups of button mushrooms (sliced)
- 6 cups of leafy green veggies like kale or spinach (rinsed, chopped)
- 1 lb of chicken thighs (boneless, skinless)
- ½ red onion (peeled, diced)
- 2 avocados
- 2 cloves of garlic (peeled)
- black pepper
- salt

Directions:

In a food processor, add the roasted peppers, garlic cloves, one of the avocados, salt, and pepper.

Blend the ingredients until you get a smooth texture for the sauce.

Transfer the sauce to a small bowl and chill in the refrigerator.

Sprinkle salt and pepper on the chicken thighs to season. Make sure to cover both sides for full flavor.

In a skillet, add the avocado oil over medium heat.

Once the oil is hot, carefully place the chicken thighs in the skillet. Cook each side of the chicken thighs for about 4 to 5 minutes.

When the chicken thighs are completely cooked through, transfer them to a cutting board and allow to rest while you cook the veggies.

In the same skillet, add the onions and cook for about 3 to 4 minutes until they start softening. Make sure to stir frequently so the onions don't stick to the pan.

Add the mushrooms and continue cooking for 2 to 3 minutes until they start softening.

Add the leafy greens then continue cooking for about 1 to 2 minutes until they start wilting.

Take the skillet off the heat then set aside.

Slice the chicken thighs into strips or bite-sized pieces. Add to the serving bowls.

Slice the remaining avocado and add to the serving bowls.

Top with a serving of the veggies and toss lightly to combine.

Add a dollop of sauce and serve immediately!

BEEF AND VEGGIE RAGU

This is a flavorful dish that's healthy, Paleo-friendly, and is a great way for you to sneak more veggies into your children's diets. This quick recipe is for ragu, a type of Italian sauce that can be poured over different kinds of pasta. If you have any leftover sauce, place it in an air-tight container and store it in the refrigerator for up to five days.

Serving Size: 6 servings

Time: 30 minutes

Prep Time: 10 minutes

Cook Time: 20 minutes

Ingredients:

- 1 tsp olive oil
- ¼ cup of basil (fresh, chopped)
- ¼ cup of mushrooms (minced)
- ½ cup of chicken broth
- 3 cups of marinara sauce (preferably tomato-basil blend)
- 1 lb ground beef (preferably grass-fed)
- 1 celery rib (minced)

- 1 large carrot (peeled, minced, you can also use baby carrots)
- 1 onion (minced)
- 3 cloves of garlic (minced)
- black pepper
- pasta (cooked, enough for 4 to 6 servings)
- salt

Directions:

In a skillet, add the olive oil over medium heat.

Add the ground beef, then cook until it starts turning brown.

Once the ground beef starts to brown, add the garlic and onions. Add some salt and pepper then continue cooking for about 2 to 3 more minutes.

Add the mushrooms, celery, and carrot to the skillet, then taste the mixture and add more salt and pepper as needed.

When the veggies are tender and the ground beef is completely cooked through, add the chicken broth and marinara sauce.

Stir the sauce well to combine all of the ingredients.

Turn the heat down to low, cover the skillet, and allow to

simmer for about 10 minutes. Stir the mixture once in a while.

After simmering, add the basil and stir to combine. Taste the sauce again and add more salt and pepper according to your preference.

Serve hot over your choice of cooked noodles. You can even use spaghetti squash to make this dish even healthier.

SAVORY STUFFED AVOCADOS

Avocados are one of the healthiest foods on the planet. This is why you can see avocados in the list of recommended foods on virtually every diet around the world. On their own, avocados might not be too appealing to children, especially since they don't have a lot of flavor. But when you add the right ingredients to it, whether sweet or savory, avocado dishes are an amazingly healthy addition to your child's Paleo journey.

Serving Size: 8 servings

Time: 25 minutes

Prep Time: 15 minutes

Cook Time: 10 minutes

Ingredients for the sauce:

- 1 tbsp lime juice (freshly squeezed)
- ¼ cup of cilantro (fresh, tender stems and leaves)
- ¼ cup of olive oil
- ½ cup of avocado oil mayonnaise (homemade or store-bought)
- 1 jalapeño pepper (deseeded, stemmed)
- sea salt

Ingredients for the avocados:

- ½ tsp smoked paprika
- 1 tbsp avocado oil
- 1 lb small shrimps (raw, peeled, tails removed, deveined)
- ½ lime
- 1 large clove of garlic (minced)
- 1 shallot (minced)
- 3 champagne mangoes (also known as Ataulfo mangoes, peeled, cut into cubes)
- 3 scallions (trimmed, sliced)
- 4 Haas avocados (cut in half, pitted)
- black pepper
- sea salt
- cilantro (chopped, for serving)

Directions:

In a food processor, add the mayonnaise, lime juice, cilantro, and jalapeño and pulse to blend well.

While pulsing, pour the olive oil into the mixture in a slow and steady stream.

Add salt and pepper according to your taste, then pour the sauce into a bowl and set aside.

In a skillet, add the avocado oil over medium heat.

Once the oil is hot, add the shallots then cook for 1 to 2 minutes until the shallots start turning brown.

Add the garlic and continue cooking for about 45 seconds until the aroma comes out.

Turn the heat up to medium-high then add the shrimp one at a time. Lay out all of the shrimps in one layer.

Sprinkle salt, pepper, and paprika over the shrimps. Cook for 2 to 3 minutes.

Flip the shrimps over and continue cooking until completely opaque and cooked through.

Turn the heat off and mix the ingredients together to coat the shrimps with the seasonings, then transfer into a bowl.

Add the scallions, mango, and the juice from the lime. Taste the mixture and add salt and pepper as needed.

Use a spoon to transfer the filling into the Haas avocado halves. If you want to add more stuffing, you can scoop some of the avocado flesh out and use it for another dish.

Garnish with cilantro and serve with the aioli sauce.

MUSHROOM AND SWEET POTATO SALAD

Sweet potatoes and mushrooms? This might sound like an odd combination, but once you (and your kids) have a taste of this unique salad, you'll keep coming back for more. This Paleo-friendly salad is considered "lighter fare," so you can pair it with fried fish or roasted chicken to make a heavier meal. But it does contain enough nutrients and flavors to make it an excellent dish to support your children's health.

Serving Size: 4 servings

Time: 35 minutes

Prep Time: 10 minutes

Cook Time: 25 minutes

Ingredients for the salad:

- 1 tbsp coconut oil
- 2 tbsp olive oil
- 1 cup of walnuts (raw)
- 1 ¼ cups of sweet potato (peeled, cut into cubes)
- 1 ½ cups of button mushrooms (cut into quarters)
- 5 cups of leafy green veggies like spinach, arugula, or kale
- 1 cucumber (sliced)
- 2 small red onions (finely sliced)
- 3 slices of bacon (sliced into small pieces)
- black pepper

Ingredients for the dressing:

- 2 tbsp apple cider vinegar
- 3 tbsp olive oil
- black pepper
- pink salt

Directions:

Preheat your oven to 350 F.

On a baking sheet lined with parchment paper, add the sweet potato cubes. Drizzle with olive oil and toss lightly to coat.

Place the baking sheet in the oven then bake the sweet potato for about 20 minutes.

While the sweet potato cubes are baking, continue preparing the salad.

In a pan, add the coconut oil over medium heat.

Add the bacon pieces, onion, mushrooms, salt, and pepper then cook for 4 to 5 minutes. You'll know it is done when the bacon is fully cooked.

Once cooked, take the pan out of the heat. Set aside.

Also, take the baking sheet out of the oven then allow the sweet potato cubes to cool down.

In a bowl, add the leafy greens, cucumber, and walnuts. Add all of the dressing ingredients and toss to combine.

Add the cooked ingredients then continue tossing until everything is well-combined.

Serve the salad on its own or with a healthy protein source like chicken, beef, or fish.

SALISBURY MEATBALLS WITH MASHED CAULIFLOWER

If you have ever tried Salisbury steak before, you will surely love these small versions. Of course, your children will love them, too. This kid-friendly dish is a classic and it is completely sugar-free. If you need to cook a quick, filling meal for your family, this is a great option.

Serving Size: 6 servings

Time: 40 minutes

Prep Time: 15 minutes

Cook Time: 25 minutes

Ingredients for the mashed cauliflower:

- 2 tbsp butter (softened)
- ¼ cup of sour cream
- ½ cup of cheddar cheese (grated)
- 2 cauliflower heads (rinsed, cut into florets)
- black pepper
- salt
- water (enough to submerge the cauliflower florets)

Ingredients for the Salisbury meatballs:

- ¼ tsp black pepper
- ¾ tsp sea salt (fine grain)
- 1 tsp garlic powder
- 2 tsp onion powder
- 1 tbsp coconut aminos
- 1 tbsp ghee (or any other Paleo-friendly oil)
- 2 tbsp brown mustard
- 2 tbsp tomato paste
- ¼ cup of white mushrooms (finely chopped)
- ⅓ cup of almond flour (blanched)
- 1 ½ lb ground beef (preferably grass-fed and lean)
- 1 egg
- parsley (finely chopped, for garnish)

Ingredients for the sauce:

- 1 tsp mustard
- 2 tsp coconut aminos
- 1 tbsp ghee (or any other Paleo-friendly oil)
- 1 tbsp tapioca (you can also use arrowroot powder if available)
- ¾ cup of white mushrooms (sliced)
- 1 ½ cups of beef bone broth (divided)
- 1 onion (chopped)
- 3 cloves of garlic (chopped)

Directions:

In a pot, place the cauliflower florets. Add water and boil for about 10 minutes until soft and fork-tender.

Drain the water and transfer the cauliflower florets into a cheesecloth. Allow to cool down enough to squeeze with your hands.

Wrap the cauliflower florets inside the cheesecloth and squeeze to remove all excess water.

In a food processor, add the cauliflower florets along with the rest of the ingredients.

Pulse until smooth, then transfer the mashed cauliflower into a bowl and set aside.

In another bowl, add the ground beef, garlic powder, onion powder, almond flour, tomato paste, mustard, chopped mushrooms, coconut aminos, egg, salt, and pepper.

Use your hands to mix the ingredients well, then take portions of the mixture and form into small balls.

In a skillet, add 1 teaspoon of ghee over medium heat.

Add the meatballs and cook until browned all around.

Turn the heat down to low and keep turning the meatballs

while you prepare the sauce. This will cook the meatballs through slowly while keeping them warm.

In a pan, add ghee along with the onions over low heat. Cook for about 2 minutes until the onions turn translucent.

Add the garlic to the pan and continue cooking for 1 more minute.

Add 1 cup of broth to the pan and bring to a simmer.

Add the coconut aminos, sliced mushrooms, and mustard, then continue simmering. Stir occasionally.

In a bowl, add the remaining broth with the tapioca. Stir well until the tapioca has completely dissolved.

Add the tapioca-broth mixture to the pan, then stir well to combine.

Transfer the meatballs (which should already be fully cooked) to the pan, cover with a lid, and continue simmering for about 5 to 10 minutes. This allows the sauce to thicken.

Spoon portions of the Salisbury meatballs to plates and serve with a side of mashed cauliflower.

CRISPY BATTERED FISH

Fig. 11: Crispy Battered Fish. Pixabay, by Karolina Grabowska, 2015, https://pixabay.com/photos/fried-fish-chilli-pepper-mint-792058/ Copyright 2015 by Karolina Grabowska/Pixabay.

This dish is crispy, tasty, and completely Paleo-friendly. You can use different types of white fish and other protein sources for this dish, like chicken or pork. Here's another super-quick meal that you can serve with a side of mashed cauliflower, a hearty salad, or a comforting bowl of soup. All of these side dishes will perfectly complement the flavor and texture of this crispy battered fish.

Serving Size: 5 servings

Time: 20 minutes

Prep Time: 10 minutes

Cook Time: 10 minutes

Ingredients:

- ¼ tsp black pepper
- 1 tsp garlic salt
- 1 tsp salt
- ¼ cup of coconut flour
- ¼ cup of water (preferably sparkling water)
- ½ cup of olive oil
- ¾ cup of tapioca starch
- 1 ½ lb of Alaskan cod fillets
- 2 large eggs

Directions:

In a bowl, add the coconut flour, tapioca starch, salt, black pepper, garlic salt, water, and eggs, then mix well to combine.

Dab the Alaskan cod fillets with a paper towel to remove excess moisture. If you prefer, you can slice them in half to make crispy battered fish fingers.

In a skillet, add the oil over medium heat. Once the oil is hot, dip the Alaskan cod fillets into the batter, shake off any excess batter, and carefully place them in the skillet.

Cook one side of the fillets for about 4 minutes.

Turn the fillets over and continue cooking for about 3 to 5 minutes more. You know you have cooked them perfectly if they are crispy on the outside and flaky on the inside. Test one of the fillets with a fork and adjust the cooking time as needed.

Once cooked, transfer the fillets to a wire rack to drain excess oil while maintaining crispiness.

Serve immediately with a healthy side dish.

GRILLED STEAK SKEWERS

This dish is a complete meal in itself. It is filling, healthy, and packed with flavor. As a bonus, it can also be a fun activity to ask your children to make their own skewers if they're old enough to handle the ingredients and the skewers safely. After cooking, you can serve these steak skewers on a side salad—you can never have too many veggies in one meal!

Serving Size: 4 servings

Time: 25 minutes

Prep Time: 15 minutes

Cook Time: 10 minutes

Ingredients:

- 1 tbsp ginger (fresh, minced)
- 3 tbsp avocado oil
- ¼ cup of coconut aminos
- ¼ cup of pineapple juice (fresh)
- 1 ½ lb sirloin steak (cut into bite-sized pieces or cubed)
- 1 bell pepper (cut into cubes)
- 1 red onion (cut into cubes)
- 1 small pineapple (cut into cubes)
- black pepper
- salt
- skewers (metal or wooden)

Directions:

Preheat your grill to medium-high heat.

In a bowl, add the coconut aminos, ginger, avocado oil, and pineapple juice. Whisk well to combine, taste, then add salt and pepper according to your preference.

Thread the ingredients onto the skewers. If you are using wooden skewers, soak them in water for at least an hour first. Alternate the onion, pepper, pineapple, and steak cubes while threading them.

Use a brush to coat the steak skewers with the marinade mixture. Make sure that all of the steak skewers are generously covered with the mixture.

Place the skewers on the grill then cook them for about 8 to 10 minutes. Every 2 to 3 minutes, turn them over and brush them with more marinade.

Once cooked, transfer the steak skewers to a plate and serve immediately.

CLASSIC CHICKEN TENDERS

This recipe involves baking the chicken tenders, making them much healthier and crispier. Of course, since this is a Paleo-friendly recipe, it is made with Paleo-friendly ingredients. It is a classic dish that your children will love. If you are used to preparing processed chicken tenders for them, they might not even notice the difference!

Serving Size: 4 servings

Time: 30 minutes

Prep Time: 10 minutes

Cook Time: 20 minutes

Ingredients:

- ½ tsp black pepper
- ½ tsp garlic powder
- ½ tsp salt
- ½ tsp smoked paprika
- ½ cup of almond flour
- ½ cup of dessicated coconut (homemade or store-bought)
- 2 lbs chicken breasts (cut into strips)
- 1 egg
- olive oil (for greasing the baking sheet)
- parsley (optional, chopped, for garnish)

Directions:

Preheat your oven to 375 F and prepare a baking sheet by greasing it with olive oil.

Rinse the chicken tenders and use a paper towel to pat them dry.

In a bowl, add the egg, whisk, then set aside.

In a separate bowl, combine the dessicated coconut, almond flour, paprika, garlic powder, salt, and pepper.

Dip each of the chicken tenders in the egg and shake off any excess.

Place each of the chicken tenders in the seasoning mixture and coat fully. Make sure each chicken tender is completely and generously coated with the seasoning mixture.

Place each of the chicken tenders on the baking sheet. There should be spaces between each of the chicken tenders.

Place the baking sheet in the oven and bake the chicken tenders for 15 to 17 minutes.

Set your oven to broil then continue cooking for another 2 to 3 minutes for a crispy coating. Check the internal temperature of the chicken tenders to make sure they are fully cooked—a reading of at least 160 F.

Once cooked, take the baking sheet out of the oven then transfer the chicken tenders to a plate. Garnish with parsley if desired and serve while hot.

MIXED SEAFOOD STEW

Most types of seafood are suitable for the Paleo diet. Therefore, learning how to cook seafood dishes can make it easier for you to encourage your kids. Here's one dish that includes different kinds of seafood. It is simple, hearty, healthy, and oh-so-yummy. It is the perfect choice for a weeknight meal for your whole family.

Serving Size: 6 servings

Time: 30 minutes

Prep Time: 5 minutes

Cook Time: 25 minutes

Ingredients:

- 1 tsp kosher salt
- 1 tbsp olive oil
- 1 cup of apple juice (unsweetened)
- 1 cup of clam juice
- 3 ½ cups of tomatoes (canned or fresh, diced)
- ½ calamari (sliced horizontally)
- ½ lb clams
- ½ lb mussels
- ½ lb shrimp (raw, peeled, deveined)
- 1 bay leaf
- 1 large onion (chopped)
- 6 cloves of garlic (minced)
- ¼ cup of parsley (optional, minced, for garnish)

Directions:

In a stockpot, add the olive oil over medium-high heat.

Add the onions to the pot and cook until tender for 2 to 4 minutes.

Add the garlic, then continue cooking for 1 to 2 more minutes.

Add the tomatoes, bay leaf, salt, apple juice, and clam juice to the pot and bring to a boil.

Once boiling, lower the heat to medium and simmer for about 20 minutes.

Add the calamari, clams, mussels, and shrimp to the pot and mix well.

Cook the seafood for about 5 to 7 minutes. The shrimp should be completely cooked through, and the shellfish should have opened.

Ladle the stew into serving bowls.

Top with parsley, if using, and serve immediately.

PAN-SEARED PORK CHOPS

There is nothing more satisfying than pan-seared pork chops with a fresh side salad. If your children love pork, they will surely love this tasty dish. This simple dish comes together easily so you can make it even on the busiest days. Give it a try once, but the next time you cook this dish, you might want to increase the quantity so your children can have seconds.

Serving Size: 2 servings

Time: 30 minutes

Prep Time: 5 minutes

Cook Time: 25 minutes

Ingredients:

- 1 tsp brown mustard (either spicy or not)
- 2 tsp olive oil (divided)
- 1 ½ lbs pork chops
- 1 lemon (cut in half)
- white truffle salt

Directions:

Preheat your oven to 400 F and grease a baking sheet with 1 teaspoon of olive oil.

Season the pork chops with salt and fresh lemon juice.

In a pan, warm the olive oil over high heat.

Place the pork chops in the pan and sear then for about 3 minutes.

Flip the pork chops over, season with more salt and lemon juice, and pan-sear the other side for about 3 minutes.

Place the pan-seared pork chops on the prepared baking sheet.

Sprinkle the pork chops with brown mustard.

Place the baking sheet in the oven, then bake the pork chops for about 25 to 30 minutes. The cooking time depends on the thickness of the pork chops.

Once cooked, take the baking sheet out of the oven.

Serve the pork chops immediately with a fresh salad for a healthy, filling meal.

CRUNCHY SALMON CAKES

Salmon is a healthy, fatty fish that children should eat more of, especially on Paleo. These crunchy salmon cakes are easy to make, super delicious, and can be eaten as the main dish with a side of veggies or as an appetizer before a Paleo-friendly pasta. It is a freezer-friendly recipe, too. This means that you can whip up a large batch and store portions in the refrigerator for a few days.

Serving Size: 8 salmon cakes

Time: 25 minutes

Prep Time: 10 minutes

Cook Time: 15 minutes

Ingredients:

- ¼ tsp black pepper
- ¼ tsp kosher salt
- ¼ tsp smoked paprika
- ½ tsp garlic (minced)
- 1 tbsp coconut oil
- 3 tbsp coconut flour
- ⅓ cup of squash (mashed or puréed, you can also use pumpkin or sweet potato)
- ⅓ lb salmon (fresh, skin-off, cooked, you can also use canned salmon)
- 1 sprig of rosemary
- 2 eggs
- ¼ tsp curry powder (optional, for seasoning)

Directions:

In a bowl, mash the cooked salmon. Make sure to remove all the skin first.

Add the mashed squash and mix until well-incorporated.

Add the coconut flour to the mixture one tablespoon at a time.

Add the rosemary sprig, pepper, salt, paprika, garlic, and curry powder if desired. Mix well to combine all of the ingredients.

Add the eggs and continue mixing to create a thick batter. If the batter comes out too runny, you may add another tablespoon of coconut flour.

Divide the batter into 8 equal portions and form them into salmon fish cakes. You can also make fewer salmon cakes that are bigger.

Place the salmon cake patties on a sheet of parchment paper.

Lay another sheet of parchment paper on top of the salmon cake patties and press down to make them thinner. Stop when they are about 1 inch thick.

In a skillet, warm the coconut oil over medium-high heat.

Once the oil is hot, carefully add the salmon cakes. Make sure the salmon cakes aren't touching. If needed, cook the salmon cakes in batches.

Cook each salmon cake for 3 to 4 minutes. Flip them over then continue cooking for another 3 to 4 minutes.

Once cooked, transfer the salmon cakes to a plate lined with a paper towel to drain excess oil.

When you have cooked all of the salmon cakes, serve them immediately. These salmon cakes pair well with steamed veggies. You can also include a Paleo dipping sauce on the side

ITALIAN CALZONE

Fig. 12: Italian Calzone. Pixabay, by ignaciomeseguersocarra, 2016, https://pixabay.com/photos/calzone-pizza-food-stuffed-lunch-1681229/ Copyright 2016 by ignaciomeseguersocarra/Pixabay.

It is time for an Italian dish to amaze your children and make them feel excited. Just because your family is on Paleo doesn't mean you can't enjoy dishes like this. Although this dish takes a bit longer to prepare, that extra time will be worth it when you enjoy the calzone with your children. Of course, this means you can only cook this dish when you have time to spare. Alternatively, you can make the dough beforehand and freeze it until you are ready to cook the calzone. It is totally up to you.

Serving Size: 3 calzones

Time: 1 hour, 10 minutes

Prep Time: 30 minutes

Cook Time: 40 minutes

Ingredients for the dough:

- ½ tsp garlic powder
- ½ tsp oregano
- ½ tsp sea salt
- ½ cup of coconut flour
- ½ cup of coconut oil
- ½ cup of water
- 1 cup of tapioca flour
- 2 eggs (1 whole egg, 1 egg white and yolk separated)

Ingredients for the filling:

- ½ cup of Paleo-friendly bacon (cooked, crumbled)
- ½ cup of Paleo-friendly pepperoni slices
- 1 cup of cheddar cheese (shredded)
- 1 cup of pizza sauce (homemade or store-bought)

Directions:

In a pan, add the water, coconut oil, sea salt, garlic powder, and oregano. Mix well and bring to a boil.

Once boiling, pour the mixture into a bowl and add the tapioca flour. Mix well until the tapioca flour is well incorporated.

Let the mixture cool down for 3 to 4 minutes. Then add the whole egg, the egg yolk, and the coconut flour.

By now, the mixture will form into dough. Knead the dough for 1 to 2 minutes.

Divide the dough into 3 equal portions and roll these into balls.

Place 1 of the dough balls between 2 sheets of parchment and roll them into rectangles.

Carefully peel off the top sheet of parchment and add all of the fillings to half of the rectangle.

Fold the dough over to create a calzone and pinch the edges to seal. Repeat these steps for the other two dough balls to create calzones.

Line a baking sheet with parchment paper and place the calzones on it.

In a bowl, add the egg white and beat to create an egg wash.

Brush the tops of the calzones with the egg wash.

Set your oven to 350 F and place the baking sheet in it. Bake the calzones for 35 to 40 minutes.

Once cooked, take the baking sheet out of the oven and allow the calzones to cool down slightly.

Serve while warm and enjoy.

MINI BURGER BITES

There is something so fun about classic dishes that are shrunken down to bite-sized versions. Although your children might already love burgers, making them smaller will make these favorites even more irresistible. This is a great dish to make for your family or even serve at parties when your kids' friends come over.

Serving Size: 20 burger bites

Time: 25 minutes

Prep Time: 15 minutes

Cook Time: 10 minutes

Ingredients:

- 1 tbsp olive oil
- 1 cup of lettuce (chopped)
- 1 ½ lbs ground beef (preferably grass-fed)
- 4 pickles (sliced into 20 pieces)
- 4 slices of Paleo-friendly bacon (cooked, cut into 20 pieces)
- 10 cherry tomatoes (each cut in half)
- black pepper
- sea salt

Directions:

Preheat your griddle or grill to medium-high.

Season the ground beef with salt and pepper. Divide the ground beef into 20 equal portions and form these portions into mini burger patties.

Grease the griddle with olive oil and place the mini patties on it.

Cook one side for 2 to 3 minutes, flip the mini patties over, and cook for another 2 to 3 minutes.

Once cooked, transfer the patties to a plate.

Top each of the mini patties with a slice of bacon, some lettuce, a pickle, and half of a cherry tomato.

Secure each of the burger bites with a toothpick and serve with a side of ketchup and mustard.

POTATO CHOWDER WITH BACON AND SHRIMP

Here's a hearty and healthy soup for you to enjoy with your kids. This is the ultimate comfort food for cold weather or any season of the year. It is a Paleo-friendly dish that is chock-full of healthy veggies. Complex as this recipe may seem, it only takes half an hour to make. Isn't that amazing?

Serving Size: 6 servings

Time: 30 minutes

Prep Time: 10 minutes

Cook Time: 20 minutes

Ingredients:

- ¼ tsp sweet paprika
- ½ tsp olive oil
- ½ tsp thyme (dried)
- ¼ cup of cashew cream (you can also use heavy cream)
- 1 cup of corn (frozen or fresh, cooked)
- 4 cups of chicken stock
- 1 lb shrimp (raw, deveined)
- 1 pack of Paleo bacon
- 1 onion (minced)
- 2 carrots (chopped)
- 2 cloves of garlic
- 2 ribs of celery (chopped)
- 3 potatoes (cut into cubes)
- black pepper
- salt
- 1 tbsp parsley (fresh, for garnish)
- 1 tbsp scallions (for garnish)
- 1 sprig of thyme (fresh, for garnish)

Directions:

In an oven-safe pot, add the olive oil over medium heat. Add the bacon and cook for about 5 to 8 minutes until crispy.

Once cooked, transfer the bacon strips into a paper towel-lined plate to drain excess oils.

Drain the bacon fat from the pot, leaving about 1 tablespoon.

Turn the heat up to medium-high and add the shrimp to the pot.

Cook the shrimp for 2 to 3 minutes, flip, and continue cooking for another 2 to 3 minutes until completely cooked through.

Once cooked, transfer the shrimps to the same plate as the bacon strips to drain excess oils.

Drain all of the liquid from the pot, then add the onion and garlic over medium-high heat and cook for about 1 to 2 minutes.

Add the carrots, celery, and potatoes to the pot, and continue cooking until the potatoes start softening.

Add the paprika and thyme, then continue cooking until fragrant for 1 to 2 minutes.

Add the chicken stock and mix well to combine. Use a spatula to scrape the brown bits that form at the bottom of the pot.

Cover the pot and bring the mixture to a boil. Once boiling, turn the heat down to medium, add the corn and allow the soup to simmer for about 10 to 15 minutes.

Whisk in the cashew cream. Taste the soup and add salt and pepper according to your taste.

Ladle the soup into serving bowls then top with bacon and shrimp.

Garnish with parsley, scallions, and thyme and serve while warm.

CHIPOTLE TURKEY BURGERS WITH SWEET POTATO

These juicy burgers are high in protein, low in fat, and totally gluten-free. Your children will be surprised at how amazingly unique these burgers taste, especially if they're only used to traditional beef burgers. You can even make them ahead of time and reheat easily when it's time to eat.

Serving Size: 5 burgers

Time: 30 minutes

Prep Time: 10 minutes

Cook Time: 20 minutes

Ingredients for the burgers:

- ¼ tsp black pepper

- ½ tsp kosher salt
- ½ tsp oregano (dried)
- 1 ¼ tsp of chipotle chili pepper (ground)
- 2 tbsp olive oil
- 2 tbsp water
- ¼ cup of cilantro (fresh, chopped)
- 2 ½ cups of sweet potato (skin-on, grated)
- 1 lb ground turkey (lean)
- 1 clove of garlic (minced)

Ingredients for assembling the burgers:

- ½ cup of salsa (homemade or store-bought)
- ½ cup of sharp cheddar cheese (grated)
- 1 avocado (pitted, peeled, sliced)
- 5 burger buns (100% whole-wheat, toasted)
- sour cream (for topping, you can also use Greek yogurt)

Directions:

In a bowl, add the ground turkey, chipotle chili powder, garlic, salt, pepper, and oregano, then mix well.

Fold in the cilantro and sweet potato, and continue mixing until all ingredients are well incorporated.

Divide the mixture into 5 equal portions and form each portion into a patty.

In a non-stick pan, warm the olive oil over medium heat.

Add the patties and cook for about 2 minutes.

Flip the patties over and continue cooking for another minute.

Add the water to the pan and quickly cover with a lid.

Allow the patties to steam for about 5 minutes until completely cooked through.

For the last 2 minutes, take the lid off, top each patty with cheese, then put the lid back on for the cheese to melt.

Once cooked, place each of the patties in the burger buns and top with salsa, avocado slices, and a dollop of sour cream.

Serve immediately.

5

SNACKS YOUR KIDS WILL ENJOY

https://unsplash.com/photos/vx7JmlGDSX4/

When you start your children on Paleo, you should try to serve them Paleo-friendly snacks, too. Although store-bought snacks are convenient and readily available in stores, there is nothing healthier and more satisfying than meals that have been prepared at home. Here, you will learn fifteen simple, yummy, and quick snack recipes that you can start making right now.

The great thing about these snacks is that they are so simple that you can even ask your children to help you make them. This is an excellent opportunity to spend quality time with your kids while talking to them about the importance of healthy food and the new diet you want them to follow. Then, later, we will discuss some tips for you to follow when choosing store-bought snacks for your kids.

SAVORY BACON MUFFINS

Although muffins usually come in sweet flavors, you can also make them savory. These bacon muffins will surprise your kids and open their minds to unconventional snack options. You can even make them ahead of time, store them in the refrigerator, and reheat them when it is time for your kids to eat their snacks.

Serving Size: 6 muffins

Time: 30 minutes

Prep Time: 5 minutes

Cook Time: 25 minutes

Ingredients:

- ¼ tsp salt
- ½ tsp baking powder
- ½ tsp onion powder
- 1 tsp garlic powder
- 1 tbsp lemon juice (freshly squeezed)
- 3 tbsp butter (melted)
- ¼ cup of chives (minced)
- ¼ cup of coconut milk
- ½ cup of coconut flour
- 3 slices of bacon (thick-cut)
- 5 eggs
- cooking spray

Directions:

Preheat your oven to 350 F and grease a muffin pan with cooking spray.

In a skillet, add the bacon strips over medium heat and cook until crispy.

Once cooked, transfer the bacon slices to a plate lined with a paper towel to drain excess oil.

Allow the bacon slices to cool, then crumble them and set aside.

In a bowl, combine the butter, lemon juice, eggs, and ¼ cup of coconut milk, then mix well.

In a separate bowl, combine the onion powder, baking powder, garlic powder, coconut flour, and salt, then mix well.

Add the dry mixture to the bowl with the wet mixture and stir well.

Fold in the chives and crumbled bacon, then pour the muffin batter into the prepared muffin pan.

Place the muffin pan into the oven and bake the muffins for about 25 to 30 minutes. Use a toothpick to check if the muffins are done. Insert a toothpick into one of the muffins all the way to the middle. If it comes out clean, the muffins are cooked.

Once cooked, take the muffin pan out of the oven and allow the muffins to cool for 10 to 15 minutes before you serve them.

MEXICAN CHURROS

If you want to serve something fancy to your kids, here's a dish that fits the bill. These churros are soft and tasty, and they go well with melted cheese or melted chocolate. Of course, they are also great eaten plain. As you invite your children to help you make this dish, why don't you share with them a few facts about Mexico, too? This will make your cooking session a lot more interesting and fun.

Serving Size: 4 servings

Time: 25 minutes

Prep Time: 10 minutes

Cook Time: 15 minutes

Ingredients:

- ½ tsp baking powder
- 1 tbsp cinnamon
- ½ cup of ghee
- ¾ cup of tapioca flour
- 1 cup of almond flour (blanched)
- 1 cup of coconut sugar (very fine)
- 1 cup of water
- 3 large eggs (lightly beaten)

- coconut oil (for cooking)
- sea salt

Directions:

In a pot, add the water and ghee over medium heat and bring to a boil.

As soon as the mixture is boiling, remove the pot from the heat and add the baking powder, almond flour, and tapioca flour.

Use a wooden spoon to mix until you get a smooth ball of dough. Allow to cool.

In a mixer set to medium, add the eggs and beat until fluffy.

Fit the mixer with a paddle attachment, then add the cooled dough to the eggs little by little.

When you have added all the dough and you have a shiny, thick batter, transfer it to a bowl. Cover the batter and allow it to rest for about 30 minutes.

In a bowl, combine the coconut sugar and cinnamon, then mix well to make the cinnamon-sugar coating.

Transfer the batter into a pastry bag with a star-shaped tip.

In a pot, add the oil and heat until it reaches a temperature of 375 F. Then, carefully squeeze the piping bag to release the churros into the hot oil. Cook the churros in batches to avoid overcrowding the pot.

Fry the churros for 45 seconds to 1 minute until golden. Once cooked, transfer the churros into a plate lined with a paper towel to remove excess oil.

Dust the churros with cinnamon sugar while warm. Repeat the steps until you have used up all the batter.

Serve the churros while warm on their own or with a dipping sauce that your kids love.

CHOCOLATE-COATED COOKIE DOUGH BALLS

Fig. 14: Chocolate Coated Cookie Dough Balls. Unsplash, by amirali mirhashemian, 2020, https://unsplash.com/photos/ V8Bc1BhXGvE/ Copyright 2020 by amirali mirhashemian/Unsplash.

Even though you have to limit your children's intake of sweets, particularly artificial or refined varieties, they can still eat chocolate. For a lot of kids, this is great news! These cookie dough balls are coated with chocolate, and once your kids try them, they will surely ask for more. Not only are they fun to eat, but they're also a lot of fun to make.

Serving Size: 24 dough balls

Time: 30 minutes

Prep Time: 15 minutes

Cook Time: 15 minutes

Ingredients for the dough balls:

- 1 tsp vanilla extract
- 1 tbsp honey (raw)
- ¼ cup of mini chocolate chips
- ¾ cup of almond flour
- 1 cup of almond butter (you can also experiment with other types of nut butter)
- sea salt

Ingredients for the coating:

- 1 cup of chocolate chips (melted)

Directions:

Use parchment paper to line a baking sheet and set it aside.

In a bowl, add the vanilla extract, honey, almond flour, almond butter, and salt, then mix well.

Fold the mini chocolate chips into the cookie dough you have made.

Use a spoon to take portions of the cookie dough, roll each portion into a ball, and place on the baking sheet you have prepared.

Once you have rolled all the batter into balls, place the baking sheet into your freezer. Leave them in the freezer for at least 5 to 10 minutes.

In a microwave-safe bowl, add the chocolate chips.

Place the bowl in the microwave and heat the chocolate chips until melted.

Take the baking sheet out of the freezer.

Take the dough balls one at a time and roll them in the melted chocolate until they are completely coated.

Put the chocolate-coated dough balls back into the baking sheet when you're done.

Place the baking sheet back into your freezer for at least 5 minutes for the chocolate to set.

Serve chilled and enjoy! You can also place the rest of the dough balls in an air-tight container and store in your refrigerator for up to a week.

PIZZA ROLL-UPS

If your kids love fruit roll-ups, these pizza roll-ups will surely intrigue them. This is a delicious snack that you can easily customize by changing the ingredients according to your preferences. For instance, if you want a low-carb version of this recipe, use turkey slices instead of tortilla wraps. You can also change the fillings to keep things interesting.

Serving Size: 2 pizza roll-ups

Time: 10 minutes

Prep Time: 10 minutes

Cook Time: no cooking time

Ingredients:

- 1 tbsp tomato sauce
- 2 tbsp cream cheese

- 2 tortilla wraps (grain-free)
- 6 large pepperoni slices (Paleo-friendly)
- 2 basil leaves (fresh, optional)

Directions:

On one of the tortilla wraps, spread 1 tablespoon of cream cheese all over the surface.

Top this with half a tablespoon of tomato sauce. Spread it all over the surface, too.

Add 3 slices of pepperoni in a line down the middle of the tortilla wrap.

Add the basil leaf, too, if desired.

Start rolling the tortilla wrap from the bottom going up. Make sure to roll it tightly. To "seal" the pizza roll, add a dab of cream cheese at the edge. Repeat the steps for the other tortilla wrap.

Serve as is or cut it into 4 slices before serving.

COCONUT SUGAR & CINNAMON SNICKERDOODLES

If you're a fan of snickerdoodles, you will definitely love these Paleo-friendly ones. You can bake them during the winter for your children to enjoy with a warm cup of chocolate or at any time of the year. In fact, when the aroma of these snickerdoodles wafts around your house as you bake them, your kids might come running to see what smells so good!

Serving Size: 34 snickerdoodles

Time: 25 minutes

Prep Time: 10 minutes

Cook Time: 15 minutes

Ingredients:

- ¼ tsp salt
- ½ tsp baking soda
- 1 tsp cream of tartar
- 1 tsp vanilla extract
- 3 tsp cinnamon (ground)
- 4 tbsp coconut sugar
- ½ cup of flaxseed (ground)
- ⅔ cup of coconut oil (melted, cooled)
- ⅔ cup of honey (you can also use maple syrup)
- 1 ⅓ cups of coconut flour
- 1 ½ cups of water
- nutmeg (optional, just a pinch)

Directions:

Preheat your oven to 400 F and use parchment paper to line a cookie sheet.

In a bowl, add the water and flaxseed, mix, and set aside. This allows the mixture to thicken.

In a bowl, combine the coconut oil, vanilla extract, and honey, then mix well.

In a separate bowl, add the baking soda, cream of tartar, coconut flour, and nutmeg, if desired, then mix well.

Add the thickened flaxseed mixture into the bowl with the wet ingredients and mix.

Gradually add the dry ingredients into the bowl with the wet ingredients. Mix as you combine until you make a soft dough.

In another bowl, add the cinnamon and coconut sugar, then mix well.

Take portions of the soft dough, roll them into balls, flatten slightly, and coat them with the cinnamon-sugar.

Once coated, add the cookies to the cookie sheet. Make sure there are spaces between each of the cookies.

Place the cookie sheet in the oven and bake the snickerdoodles for about 8 to 10 minutes.

Once cooked, take the cookie sheet out of the oven and allow the snickerdoodles to cool completely before serving.

LOW-CARB CORN DOGS

Corn dogs are a classic snack that all children love, so they will be happy to know they can still eat corn dogs even while on Paleo. Serve these corn dogs on their own or with a side of condiments for your children to make them more flavorful. Either way, these savory treats will fill your kids up nicely and give them enough energy for the rest of the day.

Serving Size: 6 corn dogs

Time: 18 minutes

Prep Time: 10 minutes

Cook Time: 8 minutes

Ingredients:

- ½ tsp baking powder
- ½ tsp sea salt
- 1 tbsp honey
- 4 tbsp arrowroot flour

- ¼ cup of arrowroot flour
- ¼ cup of butter (melted)
- ¼ cup of coconut flour
- 1 cup of coconut milk
- 1 large egg
- 6 hot dogs (Paleo-friendly)
- 6 skewers (metal or wooden)
- coconut oil (for cooking)

Directions:

If needed, pre-boil the hot dogs first and place them on a plate to cool down.

Once cooled, precoat the hotdogs with ¼ cup of arrowroot flour.

In a bowl, add 4 tablespoons of arrowroot flour, baking powder, coconut flour, and salt, then mix well.

In a separate bowl, add the milk, honey, butter, and egg, then mix well.

Pour the liquid mixture into the bowl with the dry ingredients, then mix well until you get a thick batter with a smooth texture.

In a pot, heat oil over medium heat. The oil should be enough to submerge the corn dogs completely.

Skewer a hotdog and dip it into the batter completely to coat generously. Dunk the hot dog into the batter a few times to get a thick coat. If you're using wooden skewers, make sure to soak them in water for at least 1 hour first.

Drop the corn dog in the pot and cook until golden brown on all sides. Repeat these steps for the rest of the hot dogs.

Serve while hot with your child's favorite Paleo-friendly condiments.

CHOCOLATE COOKIES WITH GOJI BERRIES

These cookies are unique as they contain a yummy and healthy combination of goji berries and dark chocolate. Goji berries are very healthy and this recipe is an excellent way to introduce this fruit to your kids. This easy recipe needs a little more than half an hour to make, but the extra time is worth it once you take a bite out of one of these cookies.

Serving Size: 12 cookies

Time: 35 minutes

Prep Time: 15 minutes

Cook Time: 20 minutes

Ingredients:

- 1 tsp baking powder
- 2 tbsp arrowroot powder
- 2 tbsp cacao powder
- 2 tbsp cacao nibs
- 3 tbsp goji berries (dry)
- 3 tbsp maple syrup (organic)
- 4 tbsp coconut oil (melted)
- 6 tbsp coconut milk (unsweetened)
- ⅔ cup of almond flour (blanched)

Directions:

Preheat your oven to 350 F and use parchment paper to line a cookie sheet.

In a bowl, add all of the ingredients and mix well. You will have a slightly wet dough with this combination of ingredients.

Leave the dough in the bowl and allow to rest for 2 to 3 minutes. If the dough is still too wet after this waiting time, sprinkle 1 to 2 teaspoons of almond flour into it and mix well.

Divide the cookie dough into 12 portions. Roll each portion into a ball and flatten to form a cookie.

Place the cookies onto the cookie sheet. Make sure there are spaces between each of the cookies.

Place the cookie sheet in the oven and bake for about 20 minutes.

Once cooked, take the cookie sheet out of the oven and allow the cookies to cool down completely before serving.

HOMEMADE POP TARTS

Fig. 15: Homemade Pop Tarts. Unsplash, by Isabella and Louisa Fischer, 2019, https://unsplash.com/photos/ X2l9M6jsS7E/ Copyright 2019 by Isabella and Louisa Fischer/Unsplash.

Pop tarts are a convenient breakfast or snack option for kids. However, the ones sold in stores aren't usually Paleo-friendly. The good news is that you can make your own pop tarts at home! This recipe is easy, tasty, and highly customizable. You can ask your children to choose the filling each time you make these pop tarts so you will be sure they will eat every last crumb.

Serving Size: 2 pop tarts

Time: 28 minutes

Prep Time: 10 minutes

Cook Time: 18 minutes

Ingredients for the crust:

- ½ tsp salt
- 1 tbsp of liquid egg (make liquid egg by beating a whole egg then only using 1 tbsp of it, you can cook the rest and eat it yourself!)
- 2 tbsp maple syrup
- 4 tbsp palm oil shortening
- ¾ cup of arrowroot flour
- ¾ cup of almond flour

Ingredients for the filling:

⅓ tsp gelatin

1 tbsp coconut sugar

¾ cup of raspberries (frozen or fresh)

Ingredients for the glaze:

- 1 tbsp raspberries (mashed)
- 2 tbsp coconut milk (chilled)
- 3 drops of liquid stevia

Directions:

Preheat your oven to 350 F and use parchment paper to line a baking sheet.

In a bowl, add all of the crust ingredients and mix well to form a dough.

Roll the dough into a ball, place it in a Ziploc bag, and place the bag in your freezer for about 30 minutes to chill.

In a bowl, add all of the filling ingredients and toss to combine.

Take the dough out of the oven and roll it into a rectangle with a thickness of ¼ inch.

Use a knife to cut the dough evenly into 4 smaller rectangles.

Divide the filling mixture in half. Pour each portion into 1 of the dough rectangles, then take the other dough rectangles and use them to cover the filled dough rectangles.

Press down on the edges of the pop tarts to seal the filling inside and place the pop tarts on the baking sheet you have prepared.

Place the baking sheet in the oven and bake the pop tarts for about 18 minutes.

Once the pop tarts are cooked, take the baking sheet out of the oven.

In a bowl, add the glaze ingredients and whip to combine.

Allow the pop tarts to cool down before coating the surface with the glaze.

Serve while warm!

HEALTHY PLANTAIN CREPES

This recipe is simple, elegant, and oh-so-good. Plantains are a healthy snack option and adding them to these crepes makes it easier for children to gobble them up. Again, this is a recipe where you can add different ingredients to make things more interesting. Why don't you add healthy fillings to these crepes like blueberries or mango slices? Yum!

Serving Size: 4 crepes

Time: 15 minutes

Prep Time: 5 minutes

Cook Time: 10 minutes

Ingredients:

- ¼ cup of coconut oil
- ½ cup of coconut milk (you can also use water)
- 1 ½ cups of plantains (puréed)
- 4 eggs
- ghee (for cooking)

Directions:

In a blender, add the puréed plantains, coconut oil, coconut milk, and eggs, then pulse to combine well.

In a non-stick skillet, add ghee over medium-low heat.

Pour ¼ cup of batter into the skillet and swirl it around to create a thin and even layer.

Wait until the crepe turns brown before flipping it over to cook the other side.

Cook the other side for about ¼ of the time it took to cook the first side. Cooking crepes well takes some practice, so don't worry if you don't get it right on the first try.

Serve the crepes while warm. You can also add fillings or toppings of your choice to make this snack more filling.

FULLY-LOADED BAKED SWEET POTATO

Although baked potatoes are usually served for lunch or dinner, this one is unique. For one, you will use sweet potato instead of a white potato, and you get to stuff it with scrumptious fillings. It is a healthy, filling snack that you can also serve for breakfast if your children ask for it. Of course, you have to set aside time for making it as it does take longer to prepare and cook this dish.

Serving Size: 2 servings

Time: 50 minutes

Prep Time: 5 minutes

Cook Time: 45 minutes

Ingredients:

- 2 tsp chia seeds
- 2 tbsp almond butter (natural)
- 1 banana (sliced)
- 2 sweet potatoes (washed)
- cinnamon

- sea salt

Directions:

Preheat your oven to 375 F and use parchment paper to line a baking sheet.

With a fork, poke holes in the sweet potatoes to facilitate cooking.

Place the sweet potatoes on the baking sheet.

Place the baking sheet in the oven and roast the sweet potatoes for about 45 minutes. You want them to be fork-tender. If needed, you can continue cooking them for 10 to 15 minutes more.

Once fork tender, take the baking sheet out of the oven and allow the sweet potatoes to cool down for 5 to 10 minutes.

Right before serving, use a knife to split one of the sweet potatoes.

Sprinkle some sea salt into the opening, then add banana slices, almond butter, chia seeds, and some cinnamon. Repeat these steps for the other sweet potato.

Serve immediately after preparing.

CHOCO-CHIA PUDDING

Fig. 16: Choco-Chia Pudding. Unsplash, by Mathilda Khoo, 2020, https://unsplash.com/photos/jiaL5L-8lwc/ Copyright 2020 by Mathilda Khoo/Unsplash.

This recipe is easy, quick, and incredibly scrumptious. Since it contains chia seeds, it is super-healthy, too. It has a smooth texture, just the right amount of sweetness, and it takes only a few minutes to prepare. This means you can have a snack ready for your hungry kids in a flash. Talk about being a super mom!

Serving Size: 6 servings

Time: 5 minutes

Prep Time: 5 minutes

Cook Time: no cooking time

Ingredients:

- ⅓ cup of cocoa powder (unsweetened)
- ⅓ cup of honey (you can also use maple syrup)
- ½ cup of chia seeds
- 2 cups of coconut milk (full fat, you can also use almond milk)

Directions:

In a blender, add all of the ingredients.

Blend for about 2 minutes on high. You can also adjust the blending time to get the thickness you desire.

Pour the pudding into serving bowls or glasses.

Serve while slightly warm. You can also place it in the refrigerator to chill before serving.

HOMEMADE OREOS

While on Paleo, your children might have to give up some of their all-time favorite snacks. If your little ones love Oreos, you can whip up your own version of Paleo-friendly Oreos at home for them to enjoy. The best part is that this recipe makes 15 cookies, so you can store the rest in the refrigerator for your kids to enjoy when they have an Oreo craving.

Serving Size: 15 cookies

Time: 30 minutes

Prep Time: 20 minutes

Cook Time: 10 minutes

Ingredients for the filling:

- ½ tsp vanilla extract
- ¼ cup of maple sugar (powdered)
- ½ cup of goat milk butter

Ingredients for the cookies:

- ½ tsp vanilla extract
- 6 tbsp goat milk butter (cold)
- ¼ cup of cacao powder
- ¼ cup of coconut flour
- ¼ cup of maple syrup (or honey)
- sea salt

Directions:

In an immersion blender, combine all of the filling ingredients together and whip the ingredients until you get an extra creamy texture.

Transfer the filling to a piping bag, then place it in your refrigerator to chill.

Preheat your oven to 325 F and use parchment paper to line a baking sheet.

In a bowl, combine all of the cookie ingredients and mix well. The cookie dough you form will look like thick frosting.

Use a spoon to take portions of the cookie dough and form these into small balls.

Place the balls on the baking sheet and flatten them gently with your palms. This recipe is enough for about 30 Oreo cookie halves (15 pairs).

Place the baking sheet in the oven and bake the Oreos for 8 to 10 minutes.

Once cooked, take the baking sheet out of the oven and allow the Oreos to cool down completely before adding the filling.

Once cooled, pipe a generous amount of filling on a cookie, then top with another cookie.

Continue piping the filling until you have finished with all of the Oreos, then serve!

PALEO PB&J

Peanut butter and jelly sandwiches are a classic snack and you can make them Paleo-friendly. This recipe is another easy one and it doesn't even take half an hour to make. If your little ones are looking for something sweet and you intend to give them something healthy, too, this is one of the best options.

Serving Size: 2 servings

Time: 20 minutes

Prep Time: 10 minutes

Cook Time: 10 minutes

Ingredients:

- 1 tsp coconut oil
- ¼ cup of berries (frozen or fresh)
- 2 cups of coconut chips (toasted)
- 2 English muffins

Directions:

In a blender, add the coconut chips and blend them on high for 1 to 2 minutes until you get a thick, smooth texture. You have just made toasted coconut butter!

Pour the toasted coconut butter into an air-tight container like a canning jar. Allow to cool before covering with a lid.

In a saucepan, warm the coconut oil over medium heat, then add the berries and use a spoon to mash them.

Once warmed through, transfer the mixture to a bowl and allow to cool.

Assemble your Paleo-friendly sandwiches, then serve!

PRETZEL-DOGS

This homemade snack is fun, tasty, and a perfect option for kids on the go. Combining pretzels with hot dogs in this dish is a winner, as they complement each other wonderfully. This is a wonderful recipe for when your children are craving something savory in the middle of the afternoon.

Serving Size: 5 pretzel-dogs

Time: 1 hour

Prep Time: 20 minutes

Cook Time: 40 minutes

Ingredients for the dough:

- ½ tsp baking powder
- ½ tsp baking soda
- ½ tsp sea salt
- 2 tbsp apple cider vinegar
- ½ cup of coconut oil
- ½ cup of tapioca flour
- ½ cup of water
- 1 cup of coconut flour
- 5 hot dogs (organic, grass-fed)
- 1 large egg

Ingredients for the glaze:

- 1 tbsp coarse salt
- 2 tbsp ghee (melted)

Directions:

In a pan, add the coconut oil, apple cider vinegar, water, and salt over medium heat then bring to a boil.

Once boiling, transfer the pan to the countertop.

Add the tapioca flour, then mix for about 2 minutes until you get a wet, pasty consistency.

Add the baking powder and baking soda, then mix for about 3 seconds while the mixture is bubbling.

Add the egg and the coconut flour, and continue mixing until you form a dough. Transfer the dough to a sheet of parchment paper.

Knead the dough for about 1 minute to soften, then divide the dough into 5 equal portions. Take one portion and roll it into a long strip.

Wrap the strip around one of the hot dogs and place it on a baking sheet lined with parchment paper. Repeat these steps for the rest of the dough and hot dogs.

When you are done making all of the pretzel-dogs, brush them with ghee and sprinkle salt over each of them.

Place the baking sheet in the oven and bake the pretzel-dogs for about 35 to 40 minutes.

Once cooked, take the baking sheet out of the oven and allow the pretzel-dogs to cool down slightly before serving.

CHOCOLATE-COATED APPLE BITES

For this last recipe, I have added a fun dish for you to make with your kids. You can make this snack whenever they want something chocolatey, and also prepare it for them on Halloween. While other kids are stuffing themselves with sugary sweets, your little ones will munch on something far healthier.

Serving Size: 12 apple bites

Time: 15 minutes (chilling time not included)

Prep Time: 10 minutes

Cook Time: 5 minutes

Ingredients:

- 1 tbsp mini dark chocolate chips
- ¼ cup of lemon juice (freshly squeezed)
- ½ cup of dark chocolate (roughly chopped)
- 1 cup of water
- 2 Granny Smith apples (washed, dried)
- cashews (roughly chopped, for topping)
- rainbow sprinkles (for topping)
- walnuts (roughly chopped, for topping)

Directions:

In a bowl, add the water and lemon juice, then mix well.

With a melon baller, cut out small circles from the apples.

Place the small circles into the bowl with lemon water and set aside.

In a microwave-safe bowl, add the mini chocolate chips. Melt the chocolate chips in the microwave and use a spoon to stir until you get a smooth texture.

Line a baking sheet with parchment paper.

Drain the water from the apple circles and pat them dry.

Using a toothpick, take each of the apple circles and dip them into the chocolate.

Place the coated apple circles on the baking sheet and sprinkle with toppings of your choice.

Place the baking sheet in the refrigerator for about 30 minutes to chill before serving.

SHOULD YOU OPT FOR STORE-BOUGHT PALEO SNACKS?

For most people, the Paleo diet is all about steaks, bacon, chicken, and other types of meat. However, the Paleo diet is much more than that. As long as you know the types of food you can feed your children on this diet, you can plan their meals in the best possible way. Of course, those meals also include snacks, especially since it seems like children are always hungry.

But would it be all right for you to opt for store-bought snacks, or only feed your kids snacks that you made yourself? When it comes to Paleo-friendly snacks, both options are okay. If you have time to prepare snacks at home, that's great! But if you need a quick and convenient solution or you're not at home and your children are begging for snacks, then store-bought ones can be suitable. The key here is to choose the right types of snacks. For instance, here are some of the best options in terms of store-bought snacks:

Almond Butter

Although almond butter typically comes in jars or bottles, it is also available in squeeze packs. This is an excellent snack when your children are craving something sweet and creamy. You can also pair almond butter with fresh fruits for a more filling snack.

Almond Flour Crackers

Crackers are a great snack, too, just make sure they are Paleo-friendly. Crackers made with almond flour are perfect for Paleo and you can pair them with spreads or tuna.

Almonds

Almonds are healthy and filling but it is very easy to overeat this snack. If you want to give almonds to your kids, give them a handful in a small bowl instead of letting them have a whole bag.

Banana Chips

When buying banana chips, make sure to check the label and list of ingredients to make sure they don't contain any ingredients that aren't approved on Paleo.

Dark Chocolate

You can feed your children dark chocolate once in a while if they like the taste.

Energy Cookies

There are Paleo-cookies available that are packed with healthy ingredients like coconut, sesame seeds, and cacao, for example. Keep these cookies in your bag whenever you go out with your kids so you always have something for them to snack on.

Tortilla Chips (Grain-Free)

These chips are made with coconut or cassava flour, which means you can feed them to your children. Pair the nachos with guacamole or salsa for a more filling snack.

Jerky Sticks

If your children are craving something savory and flavorful, jerky sticks are a great option. Just read the label to make sure that they are only made with the healthiest ingredients.

Protein Bars

These chewy bars are healthy, filling, and tasty. The best part is, they are very common. You can purchase them in most specialty-food shops that offer Paleo-friendly food products.

Roasted Seaweed

Although this option isn't exactly filling, it's a great alternative to chips. If your children want something crunchy and salty, roasted seaweed will satisfy their craving. This is a low-calorie option, too.

Turkey Sticks

You can buy these in convenience and grocery stores. Turkey sticks are very simple and contain only Paleo-friendly ingredients.

Whole Fruits

When it comes to fruits, there are lots of options available. You can serve them whole or slice them to make it easier for your children to eat.

Yogurt Alternatives (Unsweetened)

If your children are asking for dairy products, you can choose those made with coconut milk. Then add some fruits or berries to give this snack a sweet taste that your children will enjoy.

When it comes to store-bought snacks, the key is to check the labels. There are many options available, but this doesn't mean that they are Paleo-friendly. Over time, choosing the right snacks becomes easier, but at the beginning of your children's Paleo journey, you might have to learn which ones are suitable.

Fig. 17: Choosing Snacks. Unsplash, by Phuong Tran, 2018, https://unsplash.com/photos/95CjPgv3TUE/ Copyright 2018 by Phuong Tran/Unsplash.

TIPS FOR CHOOSING AND BUYING STORE-BOUGHT PALEO SNACKS

While on the Paleo-diet, the most common and "traditional" snacks like pastries and chips are off-limits. But that's okay, because your children can still have snacks whenever they feel hungry in the middle of the day. Growing children need snacks, especially if they love playing and doing other physical activities.

You don't have to struggle by making sure that all of your children's snacks are homemade. There are a lot of great options available in supermarkets and convenience stores. The key is to know which ones to choose. When it comes to choosing Paleo store-bought snacks, here are some tips for you to remember:

Check the packaging.

This is one of the easiest things you can do to make sure that the snack you buy is Paleo-friendly. Since this diet is becoming more popular, food manufacturers are already producing Paleo-friendly snacks. If you see words like "Primal," "Ancestor," or "Paleo" on the packaging, then these would be suitable for your children. Some manufacturers make it super easy by adding a Paleo-Certified Symbol—a black circle with a black "P" in the middle. If the snack has this symbol, you can go for it.

Check the list of ingredients.

All snacks have a list of ingredients for parents just like you who want to determine whether or not to buy them. If the packaging doesn't contain the words you're looking for, the next thing to do is check the ingredients list. Ideally, choose the ones that only contain a handful of ingredients, all of which are easy to understand. But if the ingredient list is too long and it includes ingredients with chemical names, then you might want to put these back. As much as possible, avoid snacks that contain the following ingredients:

- artificial coloring
- baking powder
- caramel and other flavors or colors
- citric acid
- cornflour
- cornmeal
- dairy
- dextrins
- diglycerides
- gluten
- GMOs
- grains
- glucose syrup
- glycerides
- emulsifiers

- enzymes
- fat replacements
- food starch
- high-fructose corn syrup
- legumes
- malt
- maltodextrin
- modified food starch
- natural flavors
- pseudo-grains
- soy
- stabilizers
- vegetable protein
- wheat starch
- whey protein
- yeast

Even if you have been purchasing Paleo-friendly snacks, make sure to check the labels and ingredients lists often, especially if the packaging changes. Sometimes, manufacturers "upgrade" their products, and in some cases, this means the inclusion of ingredients that you want to stay away from.

Check the nutritional labels.

The information on the nutritional labels will help you find out the breakdown of nutrients in the snacks. For instance, if you see that the snack contains too much sugar, you might want to look for something else. But if it contains a good amount of protein, then that would make it a great choice for your children.

Opt for snacks that are high in healthy fats, protein, and fiber.

Aside from being healthy and Paleo-friendly, these snacks will help stabilize your children's sugar levels to avoid a sugar crash. Also, such snacks are typically filling so they will tide your children over until their next meal.

In some cases, snacks that are ~90% compliant with Paleo requirements can broaden your range of snack options. If you cannot find snacks that are completely Paleo-friendly and you don't have time to make them, then you can opt for those which almost make the cut. Also, try to balance your children's food intake throughout the day. This is why meal planning is recommended while on the Paleo diet—to make sure your children get all the nutrients they need each day.

6

BRINGING THE PALEO DIET TO LIFE FOR THE LONG RUN

Fig. 18: Fresh Produce. Pixabay, by tookapic, 2015, https://pixabay.com/photos/fruit-market-farmer-s-market-932745// Copyright 2015 by tookapic/Pixabay.

When most people hear about the Paleo diet, they immediately think it is too restrictive for adults to follow, much less children! But as you should know by now, it's entirely possible to transition your kids to the Paleo diet in a positive and long-lasting way. Recipes as simple as the ones in the last two chapters are perfect for when you want to involve your children in the cooking process. Remember that involving your kids in this activity makes them more interested in food and proper nutrition.

While the Paleo diet has its basis in the eating habits of our early ancestors, transforming this diet into a sustainable one in our modern world means that we have to take a slightly different approach. First of all, we have to acknowledge that times have changed since our ancestors roamed the earth. Instead of trying too hard to find foods and food sources that are exactly like what our ancestors ate, do your research so you can find the best and healthiest options available in your own locale. When following the Paleo diet long-term, you have to learn how to be innovative and flexible, especially when you start introducing the diet to your children.

As a parent who has already transitioned my whole family to Paleo, I can tell you that it comes with its own set of challenges, especially when you involve your kids. If your kids are used to high-carb and high-sugar foods, expect some level of resistance to this natural diet at the beginning. Also, if you have a picky eater, you will have to be especially creative so that you can come up with ways to encourage your child to follow Paleo. But with all of the great things Paleo has to offer, all the efforts you put into encouraging your kids will be well worth it.

While researching this diet, I came across a study that highlighted the fact that children who ate whole, healthy foods (the main focus of Paleo) feel more satiated (Hardman, McCrickerd, & Brunstrom, 2014). This means that as time goes by, your children may realize that the Paleo-friendly meals and snacks you give them actually make them feel more full. It might take some getting used to, but with some persistence and a lot of enthusiasm, your children will eventually learn to enjoy and thrive on this diet. To start off this chapter, here are a few tips to help you approach the introduction of the Paleo diet in a way that children will appreciate:

Explain to your children your reasons for wanting them to follow the Paleo diet. This is especially effective for older children who can already understand the importance of health and nutrition. Never force your children to follow the diet "because you said so."

Consider giving your children non-food rewards for sticking with the diet. For instance, if they agree to go Paleo for a whole day each week, you can give them an extra hour of playtime on the weekend.

Go online and search for Paleo-friendly alternatives to their favorite foods. This will make the transition a lot smoother, especially if your children see that they won't have to give up the foods that they love.

Have plenty of Paleo snacks stored at home. Since children are frequently hungry (especially the active ones), you can give them a snack whenever they ask for one while still maintaining the lifestyle approach you are promoting.

After you introduce the Paleo diet to your children, the next challenge you have to face is helping them follow it long-term. For a lot of families, this is where things fall apart, since it is much easier to go back to our old habits if we don't consciously make an effort to maintain consistency with our new eating habits.

TRANSITIONING TO PALEO THE RIGHT WAY

To ensure that Paleo becomes your family's long-term dietary approach, you must transition into it properly. It is very easy for children to be put off by this diet, especially if they feel restricted, forced, or pressured. Remember, children respond best to love and encouragement. Therefore, you should really think about the strategies to use throughout the transition period. If you feel like something isn't working, change it. If you discover a strategy that convinces your children to eat Paleo-friendly foods without a fuss, keep using that strategy. It is all about finding what's best for your children and making changes as needed. Now, let's add more strategies to your growing bank of Paleo knowledge so that your children can transition into the diet in the best way possible:

Make sure the changes you make are age-appropriate.

Children of different ages can be transitioned into the Paleo diet, but you must base your strategies on the age of your child. For instance, explaining your reasons for wanting them to start the diet is something you can do for older kids, but if you try to give the same explanation to a toddler, they might not understand what you're trying to say. The fact is, not all children will grasp why this dietary change is so beneficial. As a result, some kids might require a more gradual transition than others.

In line with this, if your child is four years old and below, you mustn't simply start them on the Paleo diet even after everything you have learned here. While all of the strategies and guidelines in this eBook can make your child's Paleo diet easier while increasing their chance of success, for young children, you must first consult with their pediatrician. Speak to your child's pediatrician about your plans to start them on the Paleo diet. If they don't approve, then you might have to wait a few years before you introduce your child to this diet. If your child's pediatrician gives you the go-ahead, ask for advice and recommendations for how to introduce the diet to your young children safely.

Start by serving familiar dishes before you make things interesting.

Remember the tip about finding Paleo-friendly alternatives to your child's favorite foods? This tip is similar but this time, it focuses on the meals you will prepare or cook for your children. For instance, in the recipes you learned in the previous chapters, you may have noticed classics like soups, burgers, pork chops, and chicken tenders. In terms of snacks, there were also familiar options like muffins, corn dogs, and pop tarts. Serving such dishes to your children, especially during the transition phase, makes things more acceptable for them. If you cook the meals on your own, they wouldn't even know that you changed the ingredients to Paleo-friendly ones.

When your children have gotten used to the diet, then you may start serving them with more interesting dishes. Even then, try to focus more on dishes that your children enjoy. For instance, if your children love fish, serve them a lot of Paleo-friendly fish dishes. Or, if they enjoy snacks, serve them Paleo-friendly snacks that are either savory or sweet.

Customizing your children's diet allows you to help them get used to Paleo without having to argue or struggle constantly about it.

Eat the rainbow!

Since children love colorful things, encourage them to eat the rainbow! This simply means that you load their plates with colorful fruits and veggies, as both food groups are suitable for the Paleo diet. Since you will be reducing your child's consumption of legumes and grains, their carb intake will mainly come from fruits and veggies, especially the starchy ones.

There are plenty of recipes that involve fruits and veggies, so encouraging your children to eat these doesn't have to be a challenge. For instance, you can use vegetable leaves for wraps with a delicious filling, you can use spaghetti squash instead of spaghetti noodles, or you can add vegetables to sauces and soups. When you blend them up, your children won't even know that they're already eating a lot of veggies! There are also some types of fruit and veggies that children can eat raw. Just make sure to wash these first before feeding them to your kids to ensure their safety. Also, fruits and veggies are very rich in the essential vitamins, minerals, fiber, and nutrients that growing children need to grow strong and healthy.

Focus on grass-fed meat and wild-caught seafood.

Obviously, our hunter-gatherer ancestors didn't eat processed seafood and meat. So, if you really want to go Paleo, you may want to focus on grass-fed meat and wild-caught seafood. These are better for the environment, and animal proteins that have been sustainably raised are healthier for your kids, too.

For one, grass-fed meat contains more omega-3 fatty acids compared to meat from animals that survived on soy and corn feed. Also, wild-caught fish contain more of the same nutrients compared to the fish raised in farms. Omega-3s are very important, as they promote the health of the brain, skin, and heart. They can even help with mood improvement. If your local supermarkets and food shops offer these options, you may consider choosing them, especially when cooking for your children.

Eliminate processed foods completely.

This part of the transition is probably the most difficult and it will take the longest amount of time. These days, processed foods are everywhere! From chips, ice cream, pretzels, sugary cereals, processed meat products, and more, these readily available food items can be bought virtually everywhere. And since these are so convenient, we have gotten used to purchasing these types of food products to give our children fast, easy meals, and snacks whenever they want.

Of course, one of your main goals in going Paleo is to eliminate processed foods from your child's diet completely. While this will take a lot of time and effort, it's entirely possible. Just maintain consistency and keep encouraging your children to opt for whole and healthy foods instead of processed or junk foods. As long as you do this in a positive way, your children's Paleo journey can be much easier.

Try to avoid added sugar as much as possible.

While on the Paleo diet, your children will be eating virtually no sugar at all. That is, except for the sugar in fruits. When cooking snacks and desserts for your children, you can also use natural sweeteners to give them the sweetness your children crave. But another goal you have on this diet is to eliminate added sugar. This means that you should eventually wean your children off sugar. For instance, if your child is fond of flavored yogurt, give them plain yogurt with natural fruit bits mixed into it. They won't even notice the difference!

Reduce your use of salt in your dishes.

Although salt makes dishes tastier and more palatable, you should gradually reduce the use of this condiment in your cooking. This can help reduce the risk of developing cardiovascular disease, along with other adverse health issues. Of course, just because you're reducing the salt you use for cooking, this doesn't mean that you and your children will have to eat bland dishes for the rest of your lives. You can still make flavorful dishes by using herbs and spices. Combining these with fresh ingredients will make for amazing meals and snacks that you can all enjoy together as a family.

When you think you're ready to "level-up," experiment with different kinds of superfoods.

It may take a few months or even a year for your children to transition completely into the Paleo diet. Consider this transition period as a learning journey for you and your children. This is when you will learn what works, what doesn't, and what changes you can make for things to become easier for you. When your children have gotten used to the diet, you can level it up by introducing superfoods to their diet.

For instance, when making a salad, use kale instead of spinach or lettuce. Or, you can mix organ meats like liver into your dishes. Don't be afraid to experiment with the diet. If you want to keep your kids interested, then you have to find ways to add variety to it. Look for new recipes, customize your own meals, and think of new ways to serve classics. This makes Paleo more sustainable for you and your family in the long run.

These actionable steps will help you help your children succeed in their Paleo diet transition. As you already know, the Paleo diet is healthy and nutrient-dense. As time goes by, you and your children will start noticing the positive changes happening in their bodies. They will have more energy, they will become healthier, and they will become happier, too—all because you made the choice to introduce this natural, healthy, and diverse diet to them.

DON'T BE AFRAID TO FAIL

Any dietary change will take time before you can say that you have incorporated it into your life—Paleo is no different. You shouldn't be afraid to fail, and you should try not to feel discouraged if it takes a while for your kids to come around. Paleo meals and snacks will take some getting used to, especially if your children are used to non-Paleo foods, and particularly the processed varieties.

To make things easier, introduce new Paleo-friendly foods as soon as possible, preferably right after you make your plan or right after you explain the diet to your children. For most children, especially the younger ones, they have to try a certain type of food a couple of times before they willingly agree to it. Even if your child blatantly rejects the food when you first introduce it, don't give up! Wait for a couple of days, then try to give the same food again.

Personally, I have experienced this with my own child. There were many Paleo foods that my child refused to eat, especially vegetables. But I kept introducing these foods to them and putting them in different dishes. Over time, my child finally agreed to give the veggies a try. Luckily, they decided when I prepared a hearty and tasty veggie dish. Now, this dish is my child's favorite, and they always ask me to prepare it at least once a month. The more your children get used to Paleo foods, the more these foods will make them feel full and satisfied.

Of course, it takes time for them to develop familiarity with Paleo foods for them to eat as much as you would like them to. At some point, you may experience challenges and failures. However, this doesn't mean that the diet is failing or that you are failing at your goals. It only means that you have to find other ways to encourage your children and put them back on track. Here are a few tips for you:

Maintain consistency.

Being consistent is one of the most important and effective things you can do for your children. Even if you start slow, make sure to maintain consistency. If you choose to set one Paleo meal and one Paleo snack each week, make sure to do this every week. Then, as you increase the frequency of your child's Paleo meals and snacks, apply these changes for the following weeks, too. If you encounter any setbacks, brush them off, learn from them, and keep going. The more consistent you are, the easier your children will adjust to the diet.

Be persistent.

Persistence is valuable, too. For instance, if your child refuses to eat one type of food, keep trying. Or, if you notice that the meal planning routine you've picked isn't working, make some changes to it. If you never give up the fight, you will never lose to it. In the same way, if you keep moving forward with this journey, you will eventually reach your goals. You can even allow yourself to take a break if you need to. Just make sure that the break you take from the diet isn't too long and that you go back to the healthy habits that you already started following. Pair your persistence with love and encouragement and you're sure to find success on the Paleo diet with your kids.

Ask your children what they want.

Another excellent way to pull yourself up after failure is by communicating openly with your children. If you feel like you're getting nowhere or all of your efforts are going to waste, talk to your children about these failures. After explaining what the Paleo diet is and why you want your kids to follow it, the next thing you can do is ask your children what they want. For instance, print out a list of foods or dishes that are Paleo-friendly. Then, when you talk to your children, ask them which foods they would like to have. Buy the foods they want or cook the dishes they request from you. Hopefully, this will make them more willing to follow the diet—because you asked them what they want.

Take things one day at a time.

Since you will take things slow, try not to worry too much about the future. Take things one day at a time. If today was a bad day, don't think that tomorrow will be one, too. Instead, make a new plan for tomorrow with the knowledge that you have learned today. In the same way, if today was a good day, try not to assume that your children will always have good days. There might be days when your children don't like any of the meals or snacks that you have planned. When you learn how to take things one day at a time, you won't feel stressed about failures. This, in turn, can help you with the next tip.

Stay positive.

Positivity is a powerful thing. With a positive mindset, you can think of wonderful ways to keep going. And when your positivity rubs off on your children, they will be more open to following the diet, too. Being positive despite failures is easier said than done. But there's no harm in trying, right?

Just like the Paleo diet, positivity is extremely beneficial, and it's good for you, too. So, despite the failures and difficulties you will experience, try to find the bright side of things.

Failures are a part of any journey, but they shouldn't make you give up. Always remember your goals and the plans you have made. Accept these failures and use them to succeed. Pretty soon, your children will learn how to deal with failures, too, and not just when it comes to their diet.

TRIAL-AND-ERROR: AN ESSENTIAL PART OF THE LEARNING PROCESS

Fig. 19: Talking to Your Child. Unsplash, by Irina Murza, 2018, https://unsplash.com/photos/yH2WMrdLMYs/ Copyright 2018 by Irina Murza/Unsplash.

So, now you know how to introduce the diet and face its challenges head-on. What else is there for you to learn? The truth is, you are just getting started. Throughout your child's Paleo journey, you will have to introduce new things, deal with failures, and celebrate successes. Just like all other journeys you plan to take, this one involves some element of trial-and-error. This means that you have to try new things to see if they work. If they work, great! But if your trials lead to errors, you have to come up with new ideas.

When it comes to children, making any dietary changes comes with special kinds of challenges. And when those changes involve something as unique as the Paleo diet, then the challenges you face will probably be unique, too. That's okay, because the lessons you will learn through your child's journey will also help you with your own transition into the Paleo diet.

At some point—especially when you reach the height of your frustration—you might feel like the diet isn't worth it, but it is. Children who are on Paleo are healthier, they have a lower risk of developing illnesses, and they even sleep better each night. With all of the health benefits this diet has to offer, you might even see the other aspects of your child's life change for the better. So, let's go through some things that can help strengthen your resolve as a parent no matter how hard things might get:

Learn through trial and error.

As a parent, only you will know what will work best for your children—and you will learn this through trial and error. The time your children need to transition into the Paleo diet will depend on how involved you are, how interested your children are, and how well you plan your strategies. For you to learn and improve, encourage your children to share their honest opinions with you.

Let them know that it's okay for them to speak up when you serve them a dish that they don't like or a dish that they really enjoyed. You can even invite your children to help you come up with plans or strategies for your whole family to follow the Paleo diet together. If you can observe the things that don't work and your children help you by communicating openly with you, it becomes easier for you to make positive changes.

Bring your kids shopping, too.

In addition to involving your children in meal planning and inviting them to cook with you in the kitchen, you can also bring them along when you go shopping. Ideally, it would go like this: you will sit down with your children to plan your family's meals for the week. Then, you will create a list of ingredients you need to prepare or cook those meals. Ask your children to help you check for leftover meals or ingredients in your refrigerator or pantry. Cross things off from your list as needed.

After this, ask your children if they want to come with you to the supermarket. Most children will agree to this. Once there, enjoy the experience with them. Visit all of the aisles in the supermarket and talk about which food items are Paleo-friendly and which aren't. You can even make a game out of it. Point out to a specific food item and ask your child if they think it's Paleo-friendly or not. Take note, it's better to use terms like "Paleo-friendly" instead of "good," "bad," or "not allowed" when referring to foods. Shopping for ingredients is a fun experience for children and it can make them feel more enthusiastic about the diet.

Be as realistic as possible.

When you started on Paleo, you likely made your own goals. When you start your children on Paleo, you may want to create a list of goals for them, too. As you brainstorm on these goals, try to be as realistic as possible. For instance, if you set a timeline for your child's transition period, don't make it too short. Since you're the one who knows your child well, think about them as you are writing these goals.

It's important to be realistic with the diet, too. Even if you know that this diet has the potential to change your child's health positively, don't expect these changes to happen right away. It takes time for your children to adjust to the diet, and it also takes time for their bodies to start changing so that they can enjoy the benefits that this diet has to offer. When you remain realistic, you won't set outrageous expectations or standards that might make you frustrated if you can't reach them. Also, being realistic allows you to paint a better picture for your children about what this diet is all about.

Make the diet work for your children.

To increase your child's success in following the diet, make it work for them—not the other way around. This is why it's recommended to start slowly, serve familiar foods first, and remain positive throughout the process. To make this diet sustainable, your child should want to follow it. They shouldn't feel like this is a punishment you are imposing every day of their lives. Just like their diet now, your child should eventually make Paleo part of their daily routine. This is the only way you can ensure that your child (and the rest of your family) will be united in this aspect of your life.

There is always hope!

Although your child's transition won't happen overnight, if you follow all of these helpful tips, they might adjust to the diet faster than you expected. The journey doesn't have to be perfect, and you may have to make a couple of compromises along the way. But as long as your child remains open to the possibility of going Paleo and you are always there to guide them, hope will always be on the horizon.

MAKING A COMMITMENT TO THE CHANGE

Just as you made a commitment to follow the Paleo diet, you should also commit to helping your children transition into this healthy, natural diet for the long-run. With a strong sense of commitment, you will feel more motivated to keep going no matter what happens. Make this commitment for the sake of your children. You know how this diet will improve their lives, so why should you give up? Here are some things to keep in mind for you to make that all-important commitment to inspire this change in your children:

Remain firm but gentle.

Remember that not all children will happily and easily accept the Paleo diet. If your child is this way, that's okay. Allow them to express themselves. But as a parent, try not to be discouraged by rejection, especially at the beginning. Stay firm but gentle. Remember that Paleo will help your children establish healthier eating patterns as a cornerstone of their lives.

Never, ever force your child.

Your goal is to encourage your children to follow the Paleo diet, not to brainwash them into it. This is why giving your child a chance to make choices is a very effective approach. As you show your children how to follow the diet, if you give them the freedom to choose once in a while and you maintain consistency, your children will soon realize why this diet is beneficial and how they can follow it.

On the other hand, if you force your child to eat Paleo foods, they might develop an aversion to the diet, even if they eat most of the foods that are allowed on this diet, anyway. If the experience becomes negative for them, there is a very small chance that this diet will be sustainable. Forcing your child to do something is never a good idea, especially when it comes to something as important as nutrition.

Avoid making special meals for your child.

If you (and your partner) are the only ones on Paleo, then you can make special meals for yourself. At the very least, you can just make small modifications to your family's meals to make them Paleo-friendly. But when you are in the process of transitioning your children to the Paleo diet, avoid making special meals for them. If the whole family is eating Paleo meals, making a different meal for your child isn't recommended. If you keep doing this, they won't feel motivated to follow the diet. Since your child knows that you will make a different meal for them, anyway, they might not even try the foods that you are encouraging them to eat.

As much as possible, stick with homemade meals and snacks.

When it comes to committing to the Paleo diet, this is the most important thing you can do for your children. No matter how busy you are, cooking all of your child's meals and snacks will help you ensure that your children are consistently following Paleo. If you're a working mom (or dad), this can be extremely difficult. If you have a busy schedule, meal planning can be a life-saver. But if you work from home or you're a stay-at-home parent, then serving homemade meals and snacks can be a lot easier for you.

Try to think about all of the commitments you have in your life right now. You have chosen to make these commitments because they will benefit your life one way or another. In the same way, making a commitment to your child's health by starting them on Paleo will be beneficial for their lives, too. Since they are too young to make this commitment, it's your responsibility as a parent to help them out.

CONCLUSION: GOING PALEO WITH YOUR FAMILY

Fig. 20: Have Fun With It. Pixabay, by studionone, 2018, https://pixabay.com/photos/salad-rabbit-play-vegetables-food-3434616/ Copyright 2018 by studionone/Pixabay.

It's time to go Paleo.

Right now, you have just finished an entire eBook that is

focused on Paleo for kids. Here, you have learned everything you need to know about making your child's Paleo journey smooth, easy, and fun. Although you might still encounter challenges along the way, you already have the knowledge and confidence to deal with these challenges. We started this eBook by learning all about the Paleo diet. This diet goes by different names and it has been around for millions of years. As you have learned, our earliest ancestors who hunted, foraged, and gathered their food followed this diet. Although the foods available to them are not available to us now, we have to make do with what we have. This means that the best thing we can do is to follow the basic concept of the Paleo diet, which is to focus on whole, natural, and healthy foods much like our ancestors did.

In the same chapter, we discussed how this diet works and what benefits to expect from following it. All in all, the first chapter helped you understand the Paleo diet more profoundly so that you can explain it to your children, too. In the next chapter, we focused on applying Paleo to children's diets. Although most parents wouldn't even think of putting their children on a diet (unless they need to), you now know that this is more of a lifestyle change to promote better health. In this chapter, you learned all the basics of preparing your child for the Paleo diet. You even learned about the most common Paleo myths and the truth behind them.

Next, we focused on encouraging your entire family to go Paleo. It is true that there is strength in numbers. If your household is on Paleo, this makes it easier to encourage your children to follow suit. As a parent, it is your job to show your children why Paleo is beneficial and how they can transition into this diet. This chapter contained valuable tips about being positive, meal planning, and leading by example. By the end of this chapter, you started to develop an idea of how you can start gradually introducing Paleo to your children.

The next two chapters were loads of fun as you learned how to make Paleo-friendly lunch and snacks. These recipes are easy, fun to make, tasty, and, of course, completely Paleo-friendly. If you want to involve your children in cooking, you can easily start with these recipes. Within these chapters, you also learned other valuable things, like the most common Paleo-friendly ingredients to use for cooking and even how to choose store-bought snacks for when you need something quick and convenient to quell hungry tummies. Yes, store-bought snacks are okay as long as you know how to choose the healthiest options.

In the last chapter, we focused on how you can make Paleo part of your life in the long-run. By this time, you won't think of it as a diet anymore. Instead, you'll see it as your healthy approach to eating. Throughout this chapter, you learned practical and effective tips to make this one-of-a-kind diet a permanent part of your life.

As you can see, I have shared with you everything you need to know about Paleo for kids. As promised, you have gained a wealth of information to help you understand this diet better and to prepare you for the next step—introducing Paleo to your children. As a parent who has successfully transitioned my family to Paleo, I can tell you that it is not just possible, it is highly enriching and fulfilling, too. Thank you so much for choosing this eBook to help you on your Paleo journey. If you could please leave a positive review for this book, you can help other parents learn what they need to help their children. Now that you have reached the end of this eBook, it is time to apply everything you have learned. Good luck, and may you have a successful, happy journey with your children.

REFERENCES

5 Common Paleo Diet Myths...Debunked. (2014, October 13). Checks and Spots. *https://checksandspots.com/lifestyle/5-paleo-diet-myths-debunked/*

30-Minute Shortcut Beef and Vegetable Ragu. (GF, DF, Paleo). (2015, February 12). Audrey's Apron. *https://audreysapron.wordpress.com/2015/02/12/30-minute-shortcut-beef-and-vegetable-ragu-gf-df-paleo/*

Baked Paleo Chicken Tenders. (2019, May 1). Erin Lives Whole. *https://www.erinliveswhole.com/baked-paleo-chicken-tenders/*

Ballantyne, S. (2012, May 3). Transitioning My Kids To Paleo. The Paleo Mom. *https://www.thepaleomom.com/transitioning-my-kids-to-paleo/*

Ballantyne, S. (2016, September 29). 4 Must-Haves for Paleo Families. The Paleo Mom. *https://www.thepaleomom.com/paleo-families/*

Baron, R. (2018, April 2). Paleo Snickerdoodles Recipe with Coconut Flour. My Natural Family. *https://www.mynaturalfamily.com/paleo-snickerdoodles-recipe/*

Baron, R. (2019, January 12). Paleo Mac and Cheese Recipe {Gluten-Free, Clean}. My Natural Family. *https://www.mynaturalfamily.com/paleo-mac-and-cheese/*

Bejelly, K. (2012, May 15). Paleo Corn Dogs. A Girl Worth Saving. *https://agirlworthsaving.net/2012/05/paleo-corn-dogs.html*

Bejelly, K. (2013a, May 27). Paleo Pretzel Dogs. A Girl Worth Saving. *https://agirlworthsaving.net/2013/05/paleo-pretzel-dogs.html*

Bejelly, K. (2013b, October 28). Paleo Calzone. A Girl Worth Saving. *https://agirlworthsaving.net/2013/10/calzone.html*

Benefits of a Paleo Diet. (2019, January 15). Diabetes. *https://www.diabetes.co.uk/paleo/benefits-of-paleo-diet.html*

Best Paleo Snacks in 2019 (n.d.). Paleo Diet for Beginners.

Retrieved June 20, 2020, from https://paleodietforbeginner.com/best-paleo-snacks/

Booth, S. (2017). Should Your Child Go Paleo? WebMD. *https://www.webmd.com/parenting/raising-fit-kids/food/features/should-kids-go-paleo#1*

Breakfast Baked Sweet Potatoes with Almond Butter. (2016, September 12). Ambitious Kitchen. *https://www.ambitiouskitchen.com/breakfast-baked-sweet-potatoes/*

Cave Babies: Raising Happy, Healthy Paleo Kids (2012, August 1). Paleo Leap. *https://paleoleap.com/paleo-kids/*

Chipotle Sweet Potato Turkey Burgers. (2015, July 8). Well Plated by Erin. *https://www.wellplated.com/sweet-potato-turkey-burger/*

Choi, J. (2016, July 31). Bacon & Chive Paleo Muffins. What Great Grandma Ate. *https://whatgreatgrandmaate.com/bacon-chive-paleo-muffins/*

Clark, J. (2015, March 16). Paleo Battered Fish Recipe. Tastes of Lizzy T. *https://www.tastesoflizzyt.com/paleo-battered-fish-recipe/*

Cotter, L. (2017, November 27). Easy Paleo Salmon Cakes. Cotter Crunch. *https://www.cottercrunch.com/easy-paleo-salmon-cakes/*

Desmond, T. M. (n.d.). How to Go Paleo With Your Family. Parents. *https://www.parents.com/recipes/healthyeating/how-to-go-paleo-with-your-family/*

Eaton, S. B., & Konner, M. (1985). Paleolithic nutrition. A Consideration of its Nature and Current Implications. The New England Journal of Medicine, 312(5), 283–289. *https://doi.org/10.1056/NEJM198501313120505*

Eaton, S.Boyd, Cordain, L., &Lindeberg, S. (2002). Evolutionary Health Promotion: A Consideration of Common Counter Arguments. Preventive Medicine, 34(2), 119–123. https://doi.org/10.1006/pmed.2001.0966

Fish and Seafood on a Paleo Diet. (2012, October 9). Paleo Leap. *https://paleoleap.com/fish-seafood-on-paleo-diet/*

Frassetto, L. A., Schloetter, M., Mietus-Synder, M., Morris, R. C., & Sebastian, A. (2009). Metabolic and Physiologic Improvements from Consuming a Paleolithic, Hunter-Gatherer Type Diet. European Journal of Clinical Nutrition, 63(8), 947–955. *https://doi.org/10.1038/ejcn.2009.4*

Grilled Steak And Pineapple Skewers. (2019, May 24). Paleo Leap. *https://paleoleap.com/grilled-steak-pineapple-skewers/*

Growing up Paleo. (2016, April 30). The Paleo Way. *https://thepaleoway.com/blog/growing-up-paleo/*

Gunnars, K. (2018). The Paleo Diet — A Beginner's Guide Plus Meal Plan. Healthline. *https://www.healthline.com/nutrition/paleo-diet-meal-plan-and-menu*

Hardman, C. A., McCrickerd, K., &Brunstrom, J. M. (2011). Children's Familiarity with Snack Foods Changes Expectations About Fullness. The American Journal of Clinical Nutrition, 94(5), 1196–1201. *https://doi.org/10.3945/ajcn.111.016873*

Health Benefits of the Paleo Diet. (2019). Brightwater Medical Centre. *https://www.brightwatermedicalcentre.com.au/health-benefits-of-the-paleo-diet.html*

Hrdlicka, J. (n.d.). Meal Planning Tips That Make Paleo Eating Easier. Shape. *https://www.shape.com/healthy-eating/meal-ideas/meal-planning-prep-paleo-diet*

Hulet, J. (2015, August 9). Back to School Paleo Recipes. The Urban Poser. *https://theurbanposer.com/back-to-school-paleo-teens/*

JAMA and Archives Journals. (2008, July 8). Early-life Nutrition May Be Associated With Adult Intellectual Functioning. ScienceDaily. *https://www.sciencedaily.com/releases/2008/07/080707161429.htm*

Jenn. (2014a, February 14). 15 Things to Expect When Going Paleo. Fit Bottomed Girls. *https://*

fitbottomedgirls.com/2014/02/15-things-to-expect-when-going-paleo/

Jess. (2013, July 17). 17 Benefits of Eating Paleo. Paleo Grubs. *https://paleogrubs.com/paleo-benefits*

Jess. (2014b, June 12). Paleo Diet Shopping List Essentials. Paleo Grubs. *https://paleogrubs.com/paleo-diet-guide/shopping-list*

Jess. (2014c, September 29). Healthy Halloween Paleo Apple Bites. Paleo Grubs. *https://paleogrubs.com/apple-bites-recipe*

Kaylie. (n.d.). Raspberry Pop Tarts. Whole Girl. *https://wholegirl.com/portfolio_page/paleo-pop-tarts/*

King, G. (2018, December 17). How to transition Toddlers & Preschoolers to a Paleo Diet. Origins Preschool. *https://www.originspreschool.org/latest-news/2018/12/17/how-to-transition-toddlers-amp-preschoolers-to-a-paleo-diet*

Krampf, M. (2015, April 15). Delicious Paleo Mexican Churros Recipe. Wicked Spatula. *https://www.wickedspatula.com/paleo-mexican-churros/*

Kubala, J. (2019, May 31). 24 Quick and Delicious Paleo Snacks. Healthline. *https://www.healthline.com/nutrition/paleo-snacks*

Levey, D. K. (2018, January 22). A Detailed Paleo Diet Food List of What to Eat and Avoid. Everyday Health. *https://www.everydayhealth.com/diet-nutrition/paleo-diet/detailed-paleo-diet-food-list-what-eat-avoid/#summary*

Lexi. (2017, October 23). Creamy Potato Chowder with Shrimp and Bacon. Lexi's Clean Kitchen. *https://lexiscleankitchen.com/creamy-potato-chowder-shrimp-bacon/*

Lin, L. (2015, August 17). Harissa Portobello Mushroom "Tacos." Healthy Nibbles. *https://healthynibblesandbits.com/harissa-portobello-mushroom-tacos/*

Macres, C. (2016, December 24). 4 Ingredient Plantain Crepes. Camille's Paleo Kitchen. *https://paleokitchen.tv/blog/amazing-paleo-plantain-crepes-4-ingredients/*

Macri, I. (2014, June 2). Paleo Diet Myths Debunked. LifeStyle. *https://www.lifestyle.com.au/health/paleo-diet-myths-debunked.aspx*

Mason, H., & Bill Staley. (2014). Tips and Tricks Guide. Primal Palate. *https://www.primalpalate.com/wp-content/uploads/2014/03/30-Day-Guide-to-Paleo-Tips-and-Tricks.pdf*

McCracken, S. (n.d.). How to Get Your Kids to Eat Paleo (Toddler Edition). Hollywood Homestead. *https://*

hollywoodhomestead.com/4-tips-to-get-your-kids-to-eat-paleo-toddler-edition/

Meat: It's More than Protein. (2015, January 22). Paleo Leap. https://paleoleap.com/meat-protein/

Mini Hamburger Bites. (2016, February 4). Paleo Leap. https://paleoleap.com/mini-hamburger-bites/

Myers, A. (2018, February 19). 5 Tips for Choosing Autoimmune-Friendly Packaged Snacks. Amy Myers MD. https://www.amymyersmd.com/2018/02/5-tips-autoimmune-friendly-packaged-snacks/

Nut-free PB&J. (2014, October 8). Coconut Contentment. http://coconutcontentment.com/2014/10/07/nut-free-pbj/

Ofer, M. (12 C.E., May 2017). Is The Paleo Diet Healthy For Children. Pete's Paleo. https://www.petespaleo.com/blogs/blog/is-the-paleo-diet-healthy-for-children

Orenstein, B. W. (2019, December 19). Paleo Diet 101: Beginner's Guide of What to Eat and How It Works. Everyday Health. https://www.everydayhealth.com/diet-nutrition/the-paleo-diet.aspx#whattoexpect

Paleo Chocolate Goji Berry Cookies. (2016, March 8). I Heart Umami. https://iheartumami.com/chocolate-goji-berry-cookies/

Paleo Diet Benefits. (2019, May 16). Irena Macri | Food Fit For Life. *https://irenamacri.com/paleo-diet-benefits/*

Paleo: Is It Right For Kids? (2014, July 1). Our Paleo Life. *https://www.ourpaleolife.com/paleo-is-it-right-for-kids/*

Paleo Mushroom Salad. (2015, May 10). KidSpot. *https://www.kidspot.com.au/kitchen/recipes/paleo-mushroom-salad/s9lb66gj?r=collection/paleorecipes.&c=x8zmuidk/Paleo%20recipes*

Paleo Oreo Cookie (aip, egg-free). (2019, January 20). Forest and Fauna. *http://www.forestandfauna.com/paleo-oreo-cookie-aip/*

Paleo Pizza Soup. (2015, November 30). Real Food with Jessica. *https://www.realfoodwithjessica.com/2015/11/30/paleo-pizza-soup/*

Paleo Shopping List: Staples & Essentials. (2013, September 9). Irena Macri | Food Fit For Life. *https://irenamacri.com/my-essential-paleo-shopping-list/*

Raising Paleo Children Tips and Tricks. (n.d.). The Paleo Diet. *https://thepaleodiet.com/raising-paleo-children*

Ramdene, H. B. (2017, March 19). The Beginner's Guide to Meal Planning: What to Know, How to Succeed, and What to Skip. Kitchn. *https://www.thekitchn.com/the-*

beginners-guide-to-meal-planning-what-to-know-how-to-succeed-and-what-to-skip-242413

Raynor, H. A., Jelalian, E., Vivier, P. M., Hart, C. N., & Wing, R. R. (2009). Parent-Reported Eating and Leisure-Time Activity Selection Patterns Related to Energy Balance in Preschool- and School-Aged Children. Journal of Nutrition Education and Behavior, 41(1), 19–26. *https://doi.org/10.1016/j.jneb.2008.03.008*

Rosen, M. (2016, October 11). One-Pan Paleo Bacon Wrapped Chicken {Whole30}. The Paleo Running Momma. https://www.paleorunningmomma.com/paleo-bacon-wrapped-chicken-whole30/

Rosen, M. (2017, February 15). Salisbury Steak Meatballs {Paleo & Whole30}. The Paleo Running Momma. *https://www.paleorunningmomma.com/paleo-salisbury-steak-meatballs-whole30/*

Runyon, J. (2014, February 13). How To Eat Paleo With Kids. Ultimate Paleo Guide. *https://ultimatepaleoguide.com/eat-paleo-kids/*

Salmon Sheet Pan Dinner. (2020, June 19). Weelicious. *https://weelicious.com/salmon-sheet-pan-dinner-recipe/*

Seafood Stew. (2020, June 19). Weelicious. *https://weelicious.com/seafood-stew-recipe/*

Setting a Good Example for Your Kids. (2015, March 31). *https://www.healthyfamiliesbc.ca/home/articles/setting-good-example-your-kids*

Simple Paleo Pork Chops. (2015, January 15). Garlic My Soul. *https://garlicmysoul.com/blog/simple-paleo-pork-chops/*

St. Pierre, B. (2018, October 18). The Paleo Problem: Examining the Pros and Cons of the Paleo Diet. Precision Nutrition. *https://www.precisionnutrition.com/paleo-diet*

Stiehl, C., & 2017. (2017, October 17). The 35 Best Paleo Snacks For Weight Loss. Eat This Not That. *https://www.eatthis.com/paleo-snacks/*

Stuffed Avocados with Shrimp and Mango. (2016, May 5). A Calculated Whisk. *http://acalculatedwhisk.com/stuffed-avocados-shrimp-mango/*

Summers, C. (2014, November 10). Debunking Common Paleo Myths. Evolve. *https://eattoevolve.com/debunking-common-paleo-myths/*

Taesha. (2016, June 13). Instant Chocolate Chia Pudding. The Natural Nurturer. *https://thenaturalnurturer.com/instant-smooth-chocolate-chia-pudding/*

The Paleo Diet® Premise. (2020). The Paleo Diet. *https://thepaleodiet.com/the-paleo-diet-premise*

The paleo diet is fuel for healthy young families. (2018, October 15). PE Sport. *https://paleoethics.com/blogs/blog-articles/the-paleo-diet-is-fuel-for-healthy-young-families*

The Paleo Diet Team. (2020, January 29). Tips for Transitioning Kids to a Paleo Lifestyle (Plus Kid-Approved.... The Paleo Diet®. *https://thepaleodiet.com/tips-transitioning-kids-paleo-lifestyle-plus-kid-approved-paleo-snacks*

Urich, R. (n.d.). Robert Urich Quotes. BrainyQuote. *https://www.brainyquote.com/quotes/robert_urich_205053*

Valente, L. (n.d.). 5 Tricks to Steal from the Paleo Diet. EatingWell. *http://www.eatingwell.com/article/285176/5-tricks-to-steal-from-the-paleo-diet/*

Winn, J., & Winn, E. (2016a, March 30). Chocolate Chip Cookie Dough Bites (GF, Dairy-Free + Egg Free). The Real Simple Good Life. *https://realsimplegood.com/chocolate-chip-cookie-dough-bites-gf-dairy-free-egg-free/*

Winn, J., & Winn, E. (2016b, August 28). Paleo Chicken Bowl (Whole30, GF + Dairy-Free). The Real Simple Good Life. *https://realsimplegood.com/paleo-chicken-bowl/*

Younkin, L. (n.d.). Paleo Dieting for Kids: Is It Safe? EatingWell. *http://www.eatingwell.com/article/290620/paleo-dieting-for-kids-is-it-safe/*

Zeybek, C., Celebi, A., Aktuglu-Zeybek, C., Onal, H., Yalcin,

Y., Erdem, A., Akdeniz, C., Imanov, E., Altay, S., & Aydin, A. (2010). The Effect of Low-Carbohydrate Diet on Left Ventricular Diastolic Function in Obese Children. Pediatrics International: Official Journal of the Japan Pediatric Society, 52(2), 218–223. *https://doi.org/10.1111/j.1442-200X.2009.02940.x*

www.ingramcontent.com/pod-product-compliance
Lightning Source LLC
Chambersburg PA
CBHW071959070526
44583CB00015B/1264